Mes FICHES COLLÈGE 4e

CYCLE 4

Anglais

Sylvie Collard-Rebeyrolle

Nada Prévot

Hatier

Édition : Véronique Dupas, assistée de Adima El Boutahiri

Maquette de principe : Studio Favre & Lhaïk

Mise en pages : les PAOistes

Illustrations : Dorothée Jost

Iconographie : Véronique Foz / Hatier Illustration

ISBN : 978-2-401-03214-9

Coche la case quand tu as révisé la fiche ou la partie ☑

SOMMAIRE

CHECK LIST

LES COMPÉTENCES CLÉS

LES OUTILS DE LA LANGUE

Le groupe nominal

Le verbe

La phrase

UN PEU DE CIVILISATION

PODCASTS

Cet ouvrage est associé à des fichiers audio, signalés par ce pictogramme 🎧 et disponibles sur le site www.hatier-entrainement.com.

COMPRÉHENSION ORALE

Comprendre un itinéraire

1

Quand quelqu'un t'indique un itinéraire, il nomme des points de repère et il utilise des verbes spécifiques qui te permettront de te diriger. Apprends à distinguer ces deux types de renseignements.

LA MÉTHODE

1. Va sur *hatier-entrainement.com* et clique sur le titre de la fiche.
2. **Lors de la 1re écoute,** essaie d'identifier les points de repère du trajet.
3. **Lors de la 2e écoute,** concentre-toi sur les indications de direction.

Avant chaque écoute, lis le bloc de questions correspondant.

PREMIÈRE ÉCOUTE

Coche la réponse qui convient.

1. Where would Lea like to go to?

❑ a. a restaurant ❑ b. a shopping centre ❑ c. a movie theatre

2. Where does Lea have to cross the street?

❑ a. at a supermarket ❑ b. at Jenny's house ❑ c. at "Jimmy's shop"

3. Lea asks the man to explain the word "lights": what does it mean?

❑ a. 
❑ b. 

❑ c. 

4. What will Lea see just before she reaches Grand Cinema?

❑ a. a school ❑ b. the post office ❑ c. the police station

DEUXIÈME ÉCOUTE

Complète les phrases suivantes.

1. "Go all the way .... this street. At the ...., turn .... At the supermarket, 'Jenny's shop', ... and turn left."
2. "Continue .... and just before the ...., take Lauren Street ...."

HELP!

- **to bother:** déranger
- **a ten-minute walk:** dix minutes à pied
- **would you mind?** cela vous dérangerait-il ?
- **glad:** heureux(-se)
- **to cross:** traverser
- **straight on:** tout droit
- **a roundabout:** un rond-point

LE SCRIPT

Voici la transcription du document audio. Écoute-le à nouveau, en t'aidant du texte si nécessaire.

Asking for directions

LEA: Excuse me, sir! I'm sorry to bother you. I would like to go to "Grand Cinema" and I'm very late. Is there a bus I can take around here?

THE MAN: A bus? No, that's not possible. But Grand Cinema is not too far, you know. It's only a ten-minute walk!

LEA: Would you mind telling me what to do?

THE MAN: Of course not. I'll be very glad to help you. Now, go all the way down this street. At the corner, turn right. At the supermarket, "Jenny's shop", cross the street and turn left. You'll see traffic lights.

LEA: Lights?

THE MAN: You know: red, yellow, green.

LEA: Oh, yes, yes, I understand.

THE MAN: Continue straight on and, just before the roundabout, take Lauren Street on your left. Walk past the post office and "Grand Cinema" is just there. Um... Easy, *n'est-ce pas?*

LEA: Uh... well... Thanks for your help but... Taxi! Taxi!

L'homme donne des points de repère à Lea et lui indique l'itinéraire en utilisant des verbes de mouvement à l'impératif. Mais ses explications sont compliquées, Lea opte finalement pour un taxi !

FOCUS

The New York City Marathon

The New York City Marathon is always on the first Sunday of November. The first race [course] was held in 1970 and the runners used to just run around Central Park. Nowadays, the race is much more difficult, as runners go through the five boroughs [quartiers] of New York: Manhattan, Brooklyn, the Bronx, Queens, and Staten Island. It is the biggest marathon in the world, with more than 50,000 finishers each year.

CORRIGÉ p.101

D'AUTRES EXERCICES : fiche 5

COMPRÉHENSION ORALE

Comprendre le résumé d'un film

2

Quand quelqu'un te parle d'un livre ou d'un film, il te résume les principaux éléments de l'histoire et te donne son avis. Entraîne-toi à cibler ces deux types d'informations.

LA MÉTHODE

1. Va sur *hatier-entrainement.com* et clique sur le titre de la fiche.
2. **Lors de la 1re écoute,** essaie de comprendre l'essentiel de l'histoire.
3. **Lors de la 2e écoute,** concentre-toi sur les adjectifs et les verbes de goût employés par Laureen pour connaître son avis sur le film.

Avant chaque écoute, lis le bloc de questions correspondant.

PREMIÈRE ÉCOUTE

Coche la réponse qui convient.

1. What is Laureen talking about?

❑ a. a comedy ❑ b. a romantic film ❑ c. a T.V. series

2. What do we know about the characters at the beginning?

❑ a. Jack is a doctor. ❑ b. Rose is rich and Jack is poor. ❑ c. Rose is old.

3. What is the dramatic turning point in this story?

❑ a. The ship sinks. ❑ b. Jack dies. ❑ c. Rose and Jack fall in love.

4. How does the film end?

❑ a. Rose and Jack survive.
❑ b. Rose is on the *Titanic* again.
❑ c. Rose imagines that she is reunited with Jack.

DEUXIÈME ÉCOUTE

Complète les phrases suivantes.

1. "*Titanic* is one of .... and I can watch it ...."
2. "I .... DiCaprio as Jack […], and I .... Winslet as Rose."
3. "I .... when the ship breaks apart."
4. "The final scene is .... too."

HELP!

- **again and again:** encore et encore
- **to fall in love:** tomber amoureux
- **to break apart:** se briser
- **impressive:** impressionnant(e)
- **on board:** à bord
- **to sink:** couler, sombrer
- **to reunite with:** retrouver

LE SCRIPT

Voici la transcription du document audio. Écoute-le à nouveau, en t'aidant du texte si nécessaire.

> ***Titanic***
>
> *Titanic* is one of my favourite films and I can watch it again and again. All the scenes are fabulous. I'm crazy about DiCaprio as Jack – well, actually I'm always crazy about DiCaprio! – and I adore Winslet as Rose. At the beginning of the movie, we discover that Jack is a poor artist and Rose a rich young woman. They fall in love on the *Titanic* and we can imagine, of course, the terrible ending. It's almost as tragic as *Romeo and Juliet*.
>
> I always cry when the ship breaks apart because it's very impressive. We can see people panicking, screaming and falling into the sea. And when the ship finally plunges and sinks, I always have the impression that I'm on board with the actors.
>
> 
>
> Unfortunately, Jack dies, but Rose lives. The final scene is beautiful: Rose is an old lady now and she's dying. She imagines herself on the *Titanic*, reuniting forever with Jack. And you know what?! I start crying again!

Laureen nous donne les éléments clés de l'histoire en suivant la chronologie du film. Elle nous dévoile également ses impressions.

FOCUS

The Great Fire of London

The Great Fire of London occurred on the 5th of September, 1666. It started in a bakery around midnight. The fire spread throughout the streets [se propagea dans les rues] and reached the medieval City of London.

It was a tragedy: more than 13,000 houses were destroyed, 70,000 inhabitants were without a home. Only six deaths were recorded [enregistrées] because there were no statistics at the time, but of course hundreds of people died.

CORRIGÉ p.101 D'AUTRES EXERCICES : fiche 5

COMPRÉHENSION ORALE

Comprendre un dialogue au sujet d'une soirée

3

Lorsque deux personnes parlent, essaie d'abord de saisir le sujet de leur conversation. Intéresse-toi ensuite à leurs réactions en étant sensible aux nuances du langage utilisé.

LA MÉTHODE

1. Va sur *hatier-entrainement.com* et clique sur le titre de la fiche.
2. **Lors de la 1re écoute,** essaie de comprendre l'essentiel de la conversation.
3. **Lors de la 2e écoute,** concentre-toi sur les réactions des personnages.

Avant chaque écoute, lis le bloc de questions correspondant.

PREMIÈRE ÉCOUTE

Coche la réponse qui convient.

1. What is the dialogue about?

❑ a. a rock concert ❑ b. a dance show ❑ c. a party

2. What do Amy and Taylor think about this festivity?

❑ a. It was very good. ❑ b. It was terrible. ❑ c. It was so-so.

3. Who are they talking about in their conversation?

❑ a. Mary in particular ❑ b. the girls in their class ❑ c. some friends

4. What is the main topic of the conversation?

❑ a. Amy is jealous. ❑ b. Taylor is in love. ❑ c. Mary is sad.

DEUXIÈME ÉCOUTE

Que signifient les phrases suivantes ?

1. "You seem so sure of yourself, Taylor!" (Amy)

❑ a. Taylor seems confused. ❑ b. Taylor seems very determined.

2. "I should have done it." (Taylor)

Taylor ❑ a. asked ❑ b. didnt' ask Mary to go out with him.

3. "What a tragedy!" (Amy)

❑ a. Amy is making fun of Taylor. ❑ b. She is sorry for him.

4. "I feel bad enough as it is!" (Taylor)

❑ a. Taylor is very ill. ❑ b. Taylor is disappointed.

HELP!

- **last night:** hier soir
- **to go out with:** sortir avec qqn
- **to wish:** souhaiter
- **embarrassed:** gêné(e)

LE SCRIPT

Voici la transcription du document audio. Écoute-le à nouveau, en t'aidant du texte si nécessaire.

Did you enjoy the party?

TAYLOR: Tell me, Amy, did you enjoy the party last night?

AMY: Oh, yes, I just loved it! I had so much fun!

TAYLOR: Me too! Everything was perfect.

AMY: And you adored dancing with Mary. Are you in love?

TAYLOR: No! Maybe! I don't know... Well, I think I am, yes!

AMY: You seem so sure of yourself, Taylor! Did you, at least, ask her to go out with you?

TAYLOR: I know I should have done it. Oh, Amy, I wish I did...

AMY: What are you afraid of?

TAYLOR: Afraid she'd say 'no' and then I'd feel so embarrassed.

AMY: How dramatic! What a tragedy!

TAYLOR: Stop it, Amy! I feel bad enough as it is!

AMY: Relax! Mary told me this morning that she likes you so much.

TAYLOR: You are a monster! Why didn't you start with that?

Le sujet de la conversation est introduit dès le début : Amy et Taylor parlent d'une soirée et d'une certaine Mary dont Taylor est amoureux. Taylor, timide, fait part de ses doutes et de ses peurs à Amy, tandis que celle-ci le taquine avec ironie.

FOCUS

What is a Prom?

The prom is a very special event for teenagers in the USA. It is a formal dance or gathering [réunion] that celebrates the end of the last year in high school. Everybody must look very elegant, girls wear beautiful long dresses and boys wear a tuxedo [un smoking].

The boys offer a corsage* to their dates, and the girls offer them a boutonnière**. During the evening, the students dance, a meal is served and a Prom King and Prom Queen may be elected.

*A corsage is a small flower arrangement that girls wear on their wrist or on their dress.
**A boutonnière is a floral decoration for men.

CORRIGÉ p.101 D'AUTRES EXERCICES : fiche 5

COMPRÉHENSION ORALE

Comprendre un débat au sujet d'un livre

4

Quand deux personnes échangent leurs avis sur un livre, chacun explique ce qu'il a aimé ou non. Repère dans le débat les points d'accord et de désaccord.

LA MÉTHODE

1. Va sur *hatier-entrainement.com* et clique sur le titre de la fiche.
2. **Lors de la 1re écoute,** essaie de comprendre le sujet de la discussion.
3. **Lors de la 2e écoute,** identifie les points d'accord ou de désaccord.

Avant chaque écoute, lis le bloc de questions correspondant.

PREMIÈRE ÉCOUTE

Coche la réponse qui convient.

1. Which hero are Emma and Ian talking about?

❑ a. Harry Potter ❑ b. Oliver Twist ❑ c. David Copperfield

2. In this particular book, the hero is :

❑ a. a child ❑ b. a teenager ❑ c. an adult

3. Why was Ian disappointed [déçu] by the book?

❑ a. The actions are slow and boring. ❑ b. The plot is too simple.

❑ c. The author changed the hero's personality.

DEUXIÈME ÉCOUTE

Coche *agrees* ou *disagrees* selon la réaction d'Emma ou de Ian, puis complète tes réponses en relevant leurs mots exacts.

1. "Much too long!" (Ian)

Emma ❑ agrees ❑ disagrees: ".."

2. "Awesome actions too." (Emma)

Ian ❑ agrees ❑ disagrees: ".."

3. "He was a real fantasy hero!" (Ian)

Emma ❑ agrees ❑ disagrees: ".."

4. "He needs a psychiatrist!" (Ian)

Emma ❑ agrees ❑ disagrees: ".."

HELP!

- **a novel:** un roman
- **a plot:** une intrigue
- **trolls:** créatures mythiques
- **to overreact:** réagir de manière excessive

LE SCRIPT

Voici la transcription du document audio. Écoute-le à nouveau, en t'aidant du texte si nécessaire.

Harry Potter and the Order of the Phoenix

EMMA: I finished reading *Harry Potter and the Order of the Phoenix*, the fifth volume of the saga. It's a great novel, I loved it!

IAN: You really think so? I didn't like it. And 870 pages?! Much too long!

EMMA: I agree with you on that point, but the plot is really interesting. Awesome actions too.

IAN: I must admit, the actions are amazing. But Rowling's story is terribly complicated and she changed Harry Potter's personality completely.

EMMA: It's true, but it's normal: he's fifteen years old now.

IAN: But... he's too real. He's human!

EMMA: What's the problem? That's why the book is so good!

IAN: I don't see it that way. He used to fight dragons, monsters, trolls, snakes... He was a real fantasy hero!

EMMA: You're right, but now he is rebellious, angry, frustrated: a teenager like you and me!

IAN: He needs a psychiatrist!

EMMA: Oh, come on! You're overreacting.

IAN: That's how I feel. Maybe the film is not as boring...

Ian et Emma échangent leurs avis : ils évoquent les aspects positifs et les aspects négatifs de l'œuvre à l'aide d'adjectifs. Chacun réagit à ce que dit l'autre en exprimant son accord ou son désaccord.

FOCUS

Oliver Twist

Oliver Twist (1839) is Charles Dickens's second novel. The story is about a young orphan mistreated [maltraité] in a "baby farm", a place destined for children who were extremely poor. Oliver escapes, but then leads [mène] a criminal life under Fagin's control...
In this novel Dickens describes the hard life that young people led in the 19th century: no home, no money, long hours of hard work...

CORRIGÉ p.101 D'AUTRES EXERCICES : fiche 5

Quiz express

Vérifie que tu as retenu les points clés des ▸ fiches 1 à 4

5

Réponds à chacun des quiz.

Compréhension orale

1 July 4th in Chicago

Rends-toi à l'adresse suivante : *https://miniurl.be/r-1c4o*.

Lis les questions puis écoute le podcast et coche les bonnes réponses. Réécoute le podcast pour compléter ou confirmer tes réponses.

1. Who is the person talking?

☐ a. Renata ☐ b. Renalda ☐ c. Renatha

2. What is she talking about?

☐ a. the 14th of July ☐ b. Independence Day ☐ c. Labour Day

3. What does she say about the weather in Chicago on that day?

☐ a. It rains a lot. ☐ b. It's nice and warm. ☐ c. It's quite cold.

4. What is there at Navy Pier on that special day?

☐ a. 

☐ b. 

☐ c. 

5. How do most Americans celebrate the birth of their Nation?

☐ a. They visit museums. ☐ b. They party and dance.
☐ c. They go shopping.

6. What does Renata like doing?

☐ a. driving around Chicago ☐ b. going to the park
☐ c. visiting family and friends

7. What do people enjoy having?

☐ a. public meetings ☐ b. barbecues ☐ c. debates

8. What is "the taste of Chicago"?

☐ a. People plan sightseeing tours in Chicago for their visitors.

☐ b. The governor of Chicago organizes a big lottery.

☐ c. Many restaurants bring their different "specialities" for people to try.

2 English breakfast

Rends-toi à l'adresse suivante : *https://miniurl.be/r-1c4q*.

Lis les questions, puis écoute le podcast et coche les bonnes réponses. Réécoute le podcast pour compléter ou confirmer tes réponses.

1. What does Sam say about "the" typical English breakfast?

☐ **a.** It is delicious! ☐ **b.** It is very popular! ☐ **c.** It is unpopular.

2. What do some people think about the English breakfast?

☐ **a.** British have this typical breakfast every morning.

☐ **b.** It consists of a roast that British have in the morning.

☐ **c.** British do not have it every morning.

3. When is it served?

☐ **a.** when people are hungry ☐ **b.** to celebrate a birthday

☐ **c.** on special occasions

4. On what particular day of the week do British people choose to have this famous breakfast?

☐ **a.** on Monday to start the week well

☐ **b.** on Saturday because they need the weekend to digest it

☐ **c.** on Sunday morning

5. What is a brunch?

☐ **a.** a big breakfast between 10 and 11 in the morning

☐ **b.** a combination of breakfast and lunch

☐ **c.** a light lunch and an afternoon snack

6. What do we not find in a typical English breakfast?

☐ **a.** 

☐ **b.** 

☐ **c.** 

☐ **d.** 

☐ **e.** 

☐ **f.** 

Reporte-toi aux corrigés p. 101-102 et calcule ton score.

Score : .../14

EXPRESSION ORALE

Parler de ses goûts

6

Lorsque tu parles de tes goûts, tu dois dire ce que tu aimes ou pas, mais aussi expliquer pourquoi.

LA BOÎTE À OUTILS

1 Utiliser des verbes de goût

▶ Voici quelques verbes et expressions utiles pour parler de tes goûts.

	dire ce que l'on aime		dire ce que l'on n'aime pas	
verbes	to adore to love to like	to enjoy to appreciate to prefer	to detest to hate	to dislike to abhor
expressions	to be crazy about (*être fou/folle de*) to be fond of (*aimer, apprécier*) to be interested in (*être intéressé(e) par*) to be keen on (*être passionné(e) de*)		I can't bear, I can't stand (*je ne supporte pas*)	

Pour dire que quelque chose ne te dérange pas, tu utilises : *I don't mind.*

▶ Les verbes et expressions de goût se construisent le plus souvent ainsi : verbe conjugué **+ nom ou V-*ing***.

I love going to the cinema but I dislike long films.

2 Exprimer un avis nuancé

Tu peux **nuancer ton avis** en exprimant une opposition ou un contraste.

although, though: *bien que*
even though, even if: *même si*
while, whereas: *alors que, tandis que*
however, nevertheless: *cependant*
and yet, but still: *et pourtant*
on the contrary: *au contraire*

MOTS UTILES

Parler de musique

- to rehearse: *répéter*
- to record: *enregistrer*
- a record: *un disque*
- a performer: *un artiste, un interprète*
- a drummer: *un batteur*
- a guitar player: *un guitariste*
- a track: *un morceau, une piste*
- a band: *un groupe*
- lyrics: *les paroles*
- the beat: *le rythme*
- the tune: *la mélodie*
- catchy: *accrocheur*
- loud: *bruyant(e), fort(e)*
- soothing: *apaisant(e)*

METTRE EN PRATIQUE

What kind of music do you like?

Écoute Laura parler de ses goûts musicaux.

First I'd like to say that I am a real music lover. I can listen to any sort of music **whereas** some of my friends can only listen to one genre.

I must admit, **however**, that **I enjoy listening** to one particular singer, James Roly. His rock songs relax me and put me in a good mood. When you think of a rock song, you immediately imagine loud drummers. **And yet**, Roly's songs are very soothing.

I simply adore his latest hit, "Please come back to me": the lyrics are catchy and full of humour. It's about his different girlfriends and how he gets crazy when they leave him. **Since I don't like** romantic songs, I find his way of describing relationships quite original and at the same time realistic.

I don't mind listening to all his albums over and over again, **even if** some of my friends **can't stand** him.
Well, each to his own! [À chacun ses goûts]

À TON TOUR !

Mona et Sacha discutent du concert qu'elles ont vu hier soir. Complète leur dialogue en utilisant les mots proposés.

band • studios • rehearse • in love • on stage • last night • scream • songs • awesome • clapped their hands

"Hey Mona, did you enjoy the concert ....?"

"Oh, yes, it was ....!"

"I really appreciate the Big Boys' ...."

"Me too. They must .... a lot to be so good!"

"I agree with you. I guess they have fantastic .... where they can work on their ...."

"Did you see how many people .... when the band came ....?"

"I was really impressed! But I will never understand why girls .... so much."

"Well, I guess it's because they are all .... with the singers."

CORRIGÉ p.102 D'AUTRES EXERCICES : fiche 10

EXPRESSION ORALE

Parler d'un projet de vacances

7

Lorsque tu décris un projet, tu fais part de tes intentions et imagines des événements futurs. Tu peux également formuler des hypothèses et des souhaits.

LA BOÎTE À OUTILS

1 Se projeter dans l'avenir

▶ Pour situer ton projet dans l'avenir, utilise des **expressions de temps**.

next summer: *l'été prochain* • in two years: *dans deux ans*
for 5 weeks: *pendant 5 semaines* • for a while: *pendant un moment*
when I grow up: *quand je serai grand(e)* • when I am 18: *quand j'aurai 18 ans...*
[attention : contrairement à « quand » en français, *when* n'est jamais suivi du futur]

▶ Utilise le **futur** et le **futur proche** (→ FICHE 35).

I will travel around the world.
Je ferai le tour du monde.
It's going to be an amazing experience.
Ça va être une expérience incroyable.
I'm going to discover other countries.
Je vais découvrir d'autres pays.

2 Parler de ses souhaits

▶ Comme en français, on exprime un souhait à l'aide du **conditionnel** (→ FICHE 36).

it would be: *ce serait* • it could be: *cela pourrait être* • I should: *je devrais*

▶ Pour formuler une hypothèse, utilise ***if*** (« si »).

if it's possible, if I can, if I have time...

▶ Tu peux aussi faire appel à des **verbes de souhait ou de désir**.

I hope to visit... *J'espère visiter...* • I wish to see... *Je souhaite voir...*
I would love (I'd love) to learn... *J'adorerais apprendre...*
I am looking forward to speaking with... *J'ai hâte de parler avec...*

MOTS UTILES

Préparer un voyage

- to plan on (+ V-ing) / to (+ BV): *projeter de*
- to intend to (+ BV): *avoir l'intention de*
- to go on holiday: *partir en vacances*
- to discover: *découvrir*
- to visit: *visiter*
- to travel: *voyager*
- to journey: *voyager*
- to tour: *faire un circuit*
- to fly: *prendre l'avion*
- to drive: *conduire*

METTRE EN PRATIQUE

Do you have plans for the summer?

Paul projette d'aller en Californie voir son ami américain, Ryan. Il espère y faire de belles découvertes et surtout pratiquer son anglais.

Next summer, I'm planning on going to California for 5 weeks.

First, I hope to meet nice people there. Then, I would like to visit exciting places. Last but not least, I want to practise my English because I need to improve my accent.

I am looking forward to visiting Las Vegas too. And if it's possible, I would also love to go surfing in the Ocean. But it will depend on my American family. I think they are going to organise something special for my birthday...

But what I mostly wish to do is meet Ryan's friends, talk to them and go out with them. That is going to be terrific.

If I have enough money, I will buy my French friends some American souvenirs. I'll try to make everybody happy. Starting with me... *bien sûr !*

À TON TOUR !

Sam explique à un ami son projet d'aller skier avec son père. Complète sa lettre avec les mots proposés.

next month • will be • going to be • to relax • planning • would love • skiing • going to go • would be • next year

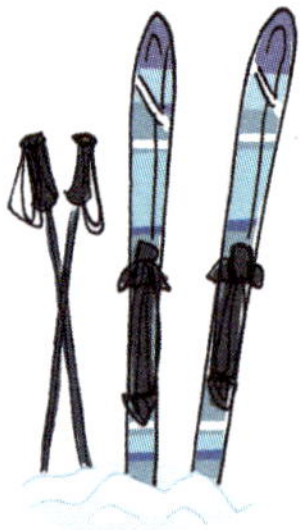

I'm really excited because, ..., I'm .... to the mountains with my Dad. We love ...., so I think we'll do that all day long!

We are also .... to visit some friends who live in the Alps: it's .... lots of fun to meet with them again.

It .... fantastic just .... and to forget all about school and homework!

I .... to ask you to come along with us, but my father says not this year.

He promised it .... for ....

Lis une première fois le texte pour savoir de quoi il parle avant de commencer à remplir.

CORRIGÉ p. 103

D'AUTRES EXERCICES : fiche 10

EXPRESSION ORALE

Demander et donner un renseignement

8

Lorsque tu t'adresses à quelqu'un dans un but précis, par exemple à un vendeur dans un magasin de vêtements, tu poses des questions ou réponds aux siennes.

LA BOÎTE À OUTILS

1 Échanger des informations

▶ Le type de renseignement demandé est indiqué au début de la question.

What size are you?
Which colour do you prefer?
How much does it cost?

▶ Pour répondre, on reprend la structure de la question ou on donne directement l'information.

What size are you? (I am) size 8.
Which colour do you prefer? (I prefer) the blue one.
How much does it cost? (It costs) seven pounds.

2 Comprendre et formuler une demande polie

▶ On utilise ***can*** pour demander la permission de faire quelque chose ou pour proposer son aide.

Can I try it on? *Puis-je l'essayer ?*
Can I help you? *Puis-je vous aider ?*

▶ On utilise ***could*** pour demander poliment un service à quelqu'un.

Could you tell me where the men's department is?
Pourriez-vous m'indiquer où se trouve le rayon Hommes ?
Could you help me find my size? *Pourriez-vous m'aider à trouver ma taille ?*

MOTS UTILES

Se renseigner dans un magasin de vêtements

- to look for: *chercher*
- to try on: *essayer*
- to fit sb.: *aller à qqn* [vêtement]
- a fitting-room: *une cabine d'essayage*
- on sale: *en solde*
- a discount: *une réduction*
- a receipt: *un ticket de caisse, un reçu*
- a suit: *un costume*
- a jacket: *une veste*
- a blouse: *un chemisier*
- a skirt: *une jupe*
- sweatpants: *un pantalon de survêtement*
- slacks, pants, trousers: *un pantalon*
- sneakers, trainers: *des baskets*

METTRE EN PRATIQUE

What would you like to buy?

Jessica veut acheter un jean pas trop cher, taille S. Elle demande conseil à une vendeuse puis se rend en cabine pour essayer le modèle choisi.

"Hello, miss. Can I help you?"
"Yes, please. I'm looking for a nice pair of jeans."
"Fine. What size are you?"
"Size small. And not too expensive, please!"
"Follow me! I'll show you our beautiful jeans on sale... 30% off."
"Very nice. I like the grey ones. Can I try them on, please?"
"Yes, naturally. The fitting-room is right here."

A few minutes later.

"So?! Do they fit you?"
"Yes, they're lovely! How much are they with the discount?"
"Twenty dollars."
"O.K. I'll take them."
"Good. How do you want to pay?"
"I'll pay in cash, please."
"Thank you. Here is your change and your receipt, have a nice day!"

À TON TOUR !

Complète le dialogue ci-dessous entre une vendeuse et son client dans un magasin de vêtements.

"...?"
"Yes, please. I'm looking for a t-shirt."
"...?"
"I'm size Large."
"O.K. .... this one ?"
"Yes, ... Can I ....?"
"Of course, the fitting-room is on your right."
"Awesome! It .... perfectly! I'll take it."

Aide-toi des réponses pour formuler les questions, et inversement.

CORRIGÉ p.103 D'AUTRES EXERCICES : fiche 10

EXPRESSION ORALE

Discuter de l'organisation d'un week-end

9

Lorsque tu discutes avec quelqu'un en vue de prendre une décision ensemble, tu dois à la fois formuler des propositions et accepter ou rejeter celles qui te sont faites.

LA BOÎTE À OUTILS

1 Faire une suggestion

Pour formuler une suggestion, on peut utiliser :

« On ne prononce pas le *l* dans *would, could* et *should.* »

– des **mots interrogatifs** ;

How about / What about (+ V-ing)? *Que dirais-tu de… ?*
Why don't we…? *Pourquoi ne pas… ?*

– des **modaux** ;

Would you like to…? *Aimerais-tu… ?*
Shall we…? *Et si nous… ?*
we could: *nous pourrions* • we should: *nous devrions*

– des **verbes de demande** (→ MOTS UTILES) ;

– de l'impératif à la 1re personne du pluriel : ***let's*** + BV.

Let's go! *Allons-y !* • Let's try! *Essayons !*

2 Accepter ou refuser une proposition

▶ **Réagis aux propositions** qui te sont faites en exprimant tes préférences.

I would love to + BV: *j'aimerais beaucoup*
I do not feel like + V-ing: *je n'ai pas envie de*
I'd rather not + BV / I prefer not to + BV: *je préfère ne pas*

▶ Tu peux également employer des exclamations idiomatiques.

How wonderful! *Que c'est merveilleux !*
What a good idea! *Quelle bonne idée !*
No way! *Pas question !*
Never ever! *Jamais de la vie !*

MOTS UTILES

Faire des propositions

- to ask, to request: *demander*
- to recommend: *recommander*
- to submit: *soumettre*
- to advise: *conseiller*
- to argue for: *plaider pour*
- to advance: *mettre en avant*
- to suggest: *suggérer*
- to persuade: *persuader*
- to influence: *influencer*
- to favour: *favoriser*
- to invite: *inviter*
- to offer: *offrir, proposer*

METTRE EN PRATIQUE

What would you like to do this weekend?

Ian et Amelia discutent des activités qu'ils pourraient pratiquer ensemble le week-end.

IAN: Hi, Amelia. Any plans for the weekend?

AMELIA: Tomorrow morning, I have my volleyball training. Why don't you come and watch me play?

IAN: OK, that's a good idea and what next?

AMELIA: Let's have lunch at that new fastfood restaurant near the Library.

IAN: That sounds good! And then?

AMELIA: Wake up, Ian! Figure something out! [Trouve une idée !]

IAN: Let me see... How about playing video games at my place?

AMELIA: Awesome! And what about Sunday?

IAN: It's homework day. I have to review all my maths lessons.

AMELIA: I need to study too. You should come to my place and we'll study together.

IAN: OK, let's do that!

À TON TOUR !

Relie les questions de Kristen aux réponses d'Abby pour reconstituer leur dialogue, puis lis l'ensemble à voix haute.

KRISTEN	ABBY
1. "What about going to the cinema?"	a. "*Monster Man*"
2. "Would you like to see *Dead Future*?"	b. "I'd rather have dinner..."
3. "What would you rather see then?"	c. "I love their spaghetti!"
4. "How about inviting Ben?"	d. "I don't like science fiction films."
5. "Let's go bowling afterwards!"	e. "Yes, everything sounds good."
6. "We should go to Pizza Parlor."	f. "That's a good idea!"
7. "It's all settled then."	g. "O.K. I don't mind."

Lis une première fois toutes les questions.

CORRIGÉ p.103 D'AUTRES EXERCICES : fiche 10

Quiz express

Vérifie que tu as retenu les points clés des fiches 6 à 9

10

Réponds à chacun des quiz.

Expression orale

1 How sporty are you?

Coche les propositions qui te correspondent, puis compte tes points.

1. I think sport is...

☐ **a.** interesting and necessary. ☐ **b.** just OK. ☐ **c.** very boring.

2. I practise sport...

☐ **a.** at school and on Saturday. ☐ **b.** every day. ☐ **c.** only at school.

3. When I practise sport, I feel...

☐ **a.** sleepy afterwards. ☐ **b.** immediately tired. ☐ **c.** good.

4. I prefer to go jogging...

☐ **a.** all alone so I can do what I want.
☐ **b.** with people who run very slowly.
☐ **c.** with people who run very fast.

5. When my father asks me to go for a bicycle ride,...

☐ **a.** I accept with joy. ☐ **b.** I pretend to be sick.
☐ **c.** I tell him: "why not? but I have a lot of homework to do..."

6. I usually work out [m'entraîne]...

☐ **a.** with my family. ☐ **b.** alone so I can stop when I'm tired.
☐ **c.** with my friends because it's more fun.

	1	2	3	4	5	6	
a	3	2	2	1	3	2	=
b	2	3	1	2	1	1	=
c	1	1	3	3	2	3	=

Total :

- 15 to 18 points: *You love sport.*
- 12 to 17 points: *Sport? with moderation...*
- 6 to 11 points: *Sport? Erk! Can I do something else, please?!*

À présent, explique ton résultat en décrivant tes comportements à voix haute à l'aide des phrases que tu as formées.

2 What do you like about your friends?

Choisis les fins de phrases qui te paraissent les plus appropriées pour parler de tes amis.

1. I have...

☐ a. many friends. ☐ b. a few friends. ☐ c. only one best friend.

2. I like my friends...

☐ a. because they are always there for me.

☐ b. because they are nice.

☐ c. because it's fun to be with them.

3. My friends must...

☐ a. be sweet with me. ☐ b. listen to me. ☐ c. understand me.

4. When I am with my friends...

☐ a. I feel great. ☐ b. I feel excited. ☐ c. I feel bored.

5. Their friendship is precious...

☐ a. because I can tell them everything.

☐ b. because I share lovely moments with them.

☐ c. because we can laugh together.

6. I love to...

☐ a. go out with my friends.

☐ b. see my friends every weekend.

☐ c. talk with my friends for hours.

7. And I also want my friends...

☐ a. to be happy in my company.

☐ b. to be nice with me.

☐ c. to trust me.

So... What do you like about your friends?

Pour répondre, lis à voix haute les phrases que tu as construites. Tu peux compléter ta réponse en ajoutant des éléments personnels.

Reporte-toi aux corrigés sonorisés sur *hatier-entrainement.com* (script p. 103).

COMPRÉHENSION ÉCRITE

Comprendre des mots inconnus dans un texte

11

Il n'est pas indispensable de comprendre tous les mots d'un texte pour en saisir l'essentiel. Mais quand des mots inconnus sont importants, comment réussir à en déduire le sens ?

LA MÉTHODE

1. Lis d'abord le texte sans t'arrêter sur les mots inconnus pour te faire une idée de son contenu. Cela te permet déjà de deviner le sens de certains mots.

2. Détermine la catégorie grammaticale du mot en fonction de ce qui l'entoure : est-ce un nom ? un adjectif ? un verbe ?

3. Observe comment le mot est construit : ressemble-t-il à un mot français ? Reconnais-tu des préfixes et/ou des suffixes ?

L'EXEMPLE COMMENTÉ

Lis ce texte au sujet des Leprechauns (prononce /'lɛprəˌkɔ:nz/), les célèbres lutins irlandais.

On St Patrick's Day, the streets of every city in Ireland (and even those of New York) are filled with Irish people celebrating their national day in tall green hats and green coats. Do you know why? Are you familiar with Leprechauns?

Leprechauns are now synonymous with Irish culture but these fairies are far from being nice little creatures. A Leprechaun is usually depicted as a trickster[1] fairy who can be mischievous, unfriendly and bad-tempered.

Traditionally, it is a solitary bearded old man wearing green and working as a shoemaker. Legend has it that[2] if you capture a Leprechaun, he will try to barter his freedom for his treasure (a pot of gold he hides at the end of a rainbow). But be careful! You must never take your eyes off him, for he can vanish in a second. A Leprechaun cannot be trusted and is likely to deceive[3] you...

HELP!

1. **a trickster:** un farceur, un arnaqueur
2. **Legend has it that...:** La légende dit que...
3. **to deceive:** tromper, duper

Dans l'introduction, le contexte évoque l'Irlande et son folklore.

- *mischievous* est suivi d'adjectif de sens négatif : c'est probablement un adjectif de sens proche (espiègle, farceur).
- *familiar* et *solitary* ressemblent à « familier » et « solitaire ».
- Dans *unfriendly* tu reconnais *friend* (ami) suivi du suffixe *-ly* (*friendly* : amical), et précédé du préfixe privatif *un-* : « inamical, peu aimable ».

OBSERVE

usually: *habituellement*
traditionally: *traditionnellement*
likely: *ici, probable*
friendly: *amical*

Le suffixe *-ly* permet le plus souvent de transformer un adjectif en adverbe, comme *-ment* en français : *usual* (habituel) + *ly* = habituellement. Mais il peut être aussi la terminaison d'un adjectif : aide-toi du reste de la phrase pour identifier la catégorie grammaticale du mot.

À TON TOUR !

1 Connais-tu le sens des mots soulignés dans le texte ? Utilise les différentes méthodes proposées pour choisir la meilleure traduction.

1. their national day: ❑ a. la nation du jour ❑ b. leur fête nationale ❑ c. le jour de leur nation
2. bad-tempered: ❑ a. par mauvais temps ❑ b. de mauvais goût ❑ c. qui a mauvais caractère
3. a shoemaker: ❑ a. un faiseur de miracles ❑ b. un cordonnier ❑ c. un marcheur
4. barter: ❑ a. troquer ❑ b. battre ❑ c. un tenancier de bar
5. treasure: ❑ a. trésorier ❑ b. trésor ❑ c. garder précieusement
6. vanish: ❑ a. disparaître ❑ b. venir ❑ c. la vanille

2 Indique si ces phrases sont vraies (TRUE) ou fausses (FALSE).

	TRUE	FALSE
1. They are Irish people.	❑	❑
2. They are supposed to live in the streets of New York.	❑	❑
3. They are playful and malicious.	❑	❑
4. They are very rich.	❑	❑
5. If you catch one of them, he'll try to trick you.	❑	❑

FOCUS

Irish folklore and fairies

Fairies are so important in Ireland that there is a special word to refer to them: 'sidhe' (pronounced *shee*). Of course, there are Leprechauns, but also Merrows and Selkies (Irish mermaids), Banshees (who announce death), Changelings (who steal human babies)...
These fairy tales and legends have their roots [racines] in ancient religions and beliefs. They are key parts of the mystery of Ireland.

CORRIGÉ p.103 D'AUTRES EXERCICES : fiche 15

COMPRÉHENSION ÉCRITE

Comprendre le récit d'une expérience personnelle

12

Lorsque quelqu'un fait le récit d'un événement, il raconte à la fois ce qu'il a vécu et comment il l'a vécu.

LA MÉTHODE

1. Identifie le contexte du récit : qui raconte son expérience ? qui sont les autres personnages ? où et quand se passe le récit ?

2. Repère les étapes du récit à l'aide des paragraphes, des mots de liaison et des expressions de temps.

3. Détermine quel est l'événement essentiel et le point de vue du narrateur en prêtant attention à la ponctuation et au lexique utilisés.

L'EXEMPLE COMMENTÉ

Lis ce que Tom se rappelle de son séjour à Malte.

Last April, everybody in my family was tired and I was really fed up with[1] my teachers and my school! We all needed a break and decided to go and spend a week in Malta.

There, we stayed in Sliema, in a nice flat overlooking[2] the harbour[3]. As soon as we arrived, we enjoyed the Seaside Promenade Walk and the typical streets of Sliema. The next day, we went to Valetta, the capital city, just across the bay. Everything was perfect!

On the third day, as the weather was sunny and warm, we decided to take a boat to Gozo and Comino, two smaller islands of the Maltese archipelago. The Blue Lagoon of Comino was just amazing! I thought I was in paradise!

But as I was there, lying on the beach and looking at the turquoise-blue sea, I heard a voice I knew too well.

"Is that you, Tom?", the voice asked.

I turned round and there she was, in her ugly swimsuit and her ridiculous flip-flops[4], looking at me with a horrible smile: Miss Cork, my English teacher!! How could she be there? This broke the spell[5] immediately... and ruined the rest of my holiday!

HELP!

1. **to be fed up (with):** en avoir marre (de)
2. **to overlook:** donner sur, surplomber
3. **a harbour:** un port
4. **flip-flops:** des tongs
5. **to break the spell:** rompre le charme

Le contexte est donné dans l'introduction : Tom raconte ses vacances en famille à Malte. Il développe ensuite son récit dans l'ordre chronologique. *But* annonce l'arrivée d'un élément perturbateur : Tom utilise alors un vocabulaire négatif et des phrases exclamatives.

OBSERVE

I was intrigued and worried. *J'étais intrigué et inquiet.*
I switched on the light. *J'allumai la lumière.*

Ne confonds pas les adjectifs ou participes passés en *-ed* et les verbes au prétérit (temps du récit). La place des premiers dans la phrase (après *be*) te permet de comprendre qu'il ne s'agit pas de verbes

À TON TOUR !

1 La phrase en italique correspond à un certain moment du récit. Repère si chaque action a lieu avant (*before*) ou après (*after*).

	BEFORE	AFTER
1. *While driving on the M1, I was trying to remember....*		
a. My great-uncle had rung at 11:30 p.m.	❑	❑
b. I decided to leave my London flat.	❑	❑
c. I parked in front of the mansion.	❑	❑
2. *After a four-hour drive...*		
a. I decided to leave my London flat.	❑	❑
b. I tried to open the door.	❑	❑
c. I walked slowly through the corridor.	❑	❑

2 Coche seulement les phrases qui correspondent au récit.

❑ **1.** The narrator's great-uncle lives in a mansion in Yorkshire.
❑ **2.** He leaves his flat to go and see him in the middle of the night.
❑ **3.** The butler is waiting for him at the door.
❑ **4.** It is silent and dark in the mansion.
❑ **5.** His great-uncle is sleeping in his armchair.
❑ **6.** His great-uncle is dead... and has probably been murdered [assassiné].

FOCUS

Detective stories

Detective fiction was established as a genre in the 19th century, with writers such as Edgar Allan Poe who inspired Arthur Conan Doyle for the most famous detective in the world: Sherlock Holmes. But the genre actually developed in the 20th century, especially in the 1920s and 30s with Agatha Christie and Raymond Chandler.

CORRIGÉ p.104 D'AUTRES EXERCICES : fiche 15

COMPRÉHENSION ÉCRITE

Comprendre un texte argumentatif

14

Dans un texte argumentatif, l'auteur cherche à nous convaincre de son point de vue. Comment, en tant que lecteur, percevoir ses arguments, son raisonnement et comprendre son opinion ?

LA MÉTHODE

1. Repère le sujet du texte grâce au titre et à l'introduction.
2. Observe l'organisation des paragraphes et les mots de liaison ou connecteurs logiques pour repérer l'articulation des idées et des arguments.
3. Déduis le point de vue de l'auteur à l'aide des arguments relevés dans l'ensemble du texte et plus particulièrement de la conclusion.

L'EXEMPLE COMMENTÉ

Lis cet article écrit par Chloe Spencer, une bloggeuse de 15 ans.

What's the point of school uniform?

A shirt, tie and blazer may not be the ingredients for my favourite outfit[1], but if I were given the choice, I wouldn't throw away[2] the idea of school uniform. Wearing a uniform is a badge of pride, creates an identity for a school and is an important part of being a school student. [...]

Some people believe that a school uniform can improve learning by reducing distraction, sharpening focus on schoolwork and making the classroom a more serious environment, allowing students to perform better academically[3].

Perhaps most importantly, a uniform means students don't have to worry about peer pressure[4] when it comes to their clothes. [...]. Potential bullies[5] have one less target for their insults; it's hard to make fun of what someone is wearing when you're dressed exactly the same.

My uniform might not be what I would wear in my own time, but it gives me a sense of belonging[6], takes away the pressure of what to wear and deters[7] the bullies. School uniform isn't fashionable, but that's exactly why I think it should be here to stay.

■ www.theguardian.com, (oct. 2013), © *Guardian News & Media* Ltd 2017.

HELP!

1. **an outfit:** une tenue
2. **to throw away:** se débarrasser de
3. **academically:** sur le plan scolaire
4. **peer pressure:** la pression du groupe
5. **a bully:** un tyran (qui harcèle ou malmène les autres)
6. **a sense of belonging:** un sentiment d'appartenance
7. **to deter:** dissuader

Chloe Spencer liste des arguments en faveur de l'uniforme à l'école, du plus superficiel au plus important. La conclusion résume son opinion : l'uniforme doit être conservé.

OBSERVE

Wearing a uniform: *porter un uniforme* • by reducing: *en réduisant*
What someone is wearing: *ce que quelqu'un porte*

Ne confonds pas la forme progressive *be* + V-*ing* avec V-*ing* seul, que l'on rencontre en position de sujet ou après une préposition. Il se traduit le plus souvent par un participe présent ou un infinitif.

À TON TOUR !

1 Coche les affirmations correspondant à ce que pense Chloe de l'uniforme à l'école.

- ❑ **1.** Wearing a uniform makes you feel you are a school student.
- ❑ **2.** It makes it difficult for school students to focus on schoolwork.
- ❑ **3.** It allows students to work in better conditions.
- ❑ **4.** It helps students have better grades and results at school.
- ❑ **5.** It deters bullies from mocking other students' clothes.
- ❑ **6.** It prevents [empêche de] students from worrying about their clothes.
- ❑ **7.** It is what Chloe likes wearing in her free time.
- ❑ **8.** It is usually beautiful and trendy [tendance, à la mode].
- ❑ **9.** It shouldn't be abandoned in British schools.

2 Parmi les arguments ci-dessus, quels sont les plus importants selon Chloe ? Note les numéros correspondants.

According to Chloe, the main arguments are : .... and ....

FOCUS

School uniforms in the UK

Uniforms were introduced in British schools in the 16th century, first at charity schools for poor children. Later, they became associated with the upper class when "public schools" (student selective, private and expensive secondary schools) began to use them. Nowadays, uniforms are obligatory in most elementary and secondary schools in the UK. Each school has its own rules about its school uniforms, and they are usually strict!

CORRIGÉ p.104 D'AUTRES EXERCICES : fiche 15

Quiz express

Vérifie que tu as retenu les points clés des fiches 11 à 14

15

Réponds à chacun des quiz, puis résous l'énigme.

Compréhension écrite

"He should have been back by eleven thirty," said the voice on the phone. "I'm so worried. It's the first time he's been out with the car at night."
"And how old did you say your son is?" asked Sergeant Parker.
"Seventeen, officer. He only passed his test a week ago. And Melanie's only 15."
"Well, Mrs. Hoskins, I can only say that I haven't had any reports of incidents involving[1] a blue Escort; but I'll put out a message. Just make sure you call us back immediately if he comes home. We can't afford to waste[2] police time, can we?"
"No, officer, of course not. But you'll let us know at once if you find them, won't you?"
"Yes Ma'am, we will."
Parker looked at the clock on the wall. It was just after two.
"Constable Shepton!"
"Sir?"
"Put out a message to all cars. Look out for a dark blue Escort, registration number J47 HGK. Driver's a young lad[3] of 17 called Paul Hoskins – just passed his test. His mum expected him home before midnight. Hasn't shown up[4]."

1. involving: *concernant* ; 2. to waste (time): *gâcher, perdre (du temps)* ;
3. a lad: *un gars, un gamin* ; 4. to show up: *arriver, se pointer.*

1 Comprendre les mots inconnus

Entoure la nature des mots puis coche leur traduction.

1. *foggy*: adjectif • adverbe • nom

☐ **a.** brumeux (-se) ☐ **b.** solitaire ☐ **c.** agité(e) ☐ **d.** calme

2. *worried*: adjectif • adverbe • verbe

☐ **a.** marié(e) ☐ **b.** guerrier ☐ **c.** inquiet(-ète) ☐ **d.** surpris(e)

3. *passed (his test)*: adjectif • nom • verbe

☐ **a.** passé ☐ **b.** a passé ☐ **c.** a réussi ☐ **d.** réussite

4. *constable*: adjectif • adverbe • nom

☐ **a.** agent de police ☐ **b.** constatation ☐ **c.** constant(e)

5. *registration number* : adjectif • adverbe • nom

☐ **a.** numéro de registre ☐ **b.** numéro d'immatriculation

2 Comprendre les informations essentielles

Coche la ou les propositions qui conviennent.

1. The scene takes place...

☐ **a.** during the day ☐ **b.** in the afternoon ☐ **c.** at night
☐ **d.** at a police station ☐ **e.** in a car ☐ **f.** at Mrs Hoskins' house.

2. The characters who are speaking are...

☐ **a.** Sergeant Parker ☐ **b.** Mrs Hoskins ☐ **c.** Paul
☐ **d.** Melanie ☐ **e.** Constable Shepton

3. They are speaking about...

☐ **a.** Mrs Hoskins ☐ **b.** Paul ☐ **c.** Melanie

4. Mrs Hoskins is calling because Paul...

☐ **a.** has had an accident ☐ **b.** hasn't come back home yet.

3 Comprendre les détails

Les affirmations suivantes sont-elles vraies (*True*) ou fausses (*False*)?

	TRUE	FALSE
1. Mrs Hoskins is worried about her husband.	☐	☐
2. Paul is Mrs Hoskins's son.	☐	☐
3. Paul took Melanie out with his car.	☐	☐
4. Paul always takes his car to go out at night.	☐	☐
5. Mrs Hoskins doesn't know where Paul is.	☐	☐
6. S. Parker doesn't want to look for [chercher] Paul.	☐	☐
7. S. Parker wants to put a message to all police cars.	☐	☐

ÉNIGME

Décrypte ce message pour découvrir le titre d'un roman d'Agatha Christie, célèbre auteure de romans policiers.

13-21-18-4-5-18 15-14 20-8-5 15-18-9-5-14-20 5-24-16-18-5-19-19

_ _ _ _ _ _   _ _   _ _ _   _ _ _ _ _ _ _   _ _ _ _ _ _ _

Murder on the Orient Express

Reporte-toi aux corrigés p. 104 et calcule ton score.

Score : .../16

EXPRESSION ÉCRITE

Décrire une image

16

Quand tu décris une image, tu dois être méthodique dans ton analyse et précis(e) dans le choix de tes mots.

LA BOÎTE À OUTILS

1 Présenter le document

▶ Indique d'abord de quel **type d'image** il s'agit.

- a cartoon: *un dessin humoristique*
- a drawing: *un dessin*
- a painting: *un tableau*
- an ad(vertisement): *une pub(licité)*
- a poster: *une affiche*
- a book cover: *une couverture de livre*

▶ Donne ensuite les informations complémentaires qui accompagnent le document : **titre, auteur, date**…

It is entitled... *Il/elle s'intitule...*
It was taken/drawn/painted/created by...
Il/elle a été pris(e), dessiné(e), peint(e), créé(e) par...
in (+ year): *en (+ année)* • on (+ day): *le (+ jour)*

« La légende d'un document se dit ***caption***. »

▶ Identifie le sujet ou le **thème principal** de l'image.

It shows... *Il/elle montre...* • It is about... *Il/elle a pour sujet....*
The focal point of the picture is... *Le centre d'intérêt de l'image est...*

2 Situer les différents éléments de l'image

MOTS UTILES

Décrire une ville

- the city centre [UK] / center [US]: *le centre-ville*
- a building: *un bâtiment*
- a shop [UK], a store [US]: *un magasin*
- a street: *une rue*
- the traffic: *la circulation*
- a cross/roads: *un carrefour*
- a double-decker bus: *un bus à deux étages*
- the pavement: *le trottoir*
- a pedestrian: *un piéton*
- busy: *animé(e)*

METTRE EN PRATIQUE

Describe a painting

Voici une description de ce tableau.

West-End London Street Scene, Grace Golden (1945)

This document is a painting created by Grace Golden in 1945, at the end of World War II. It is entitled *A West-End London Street Scene* and shows a busy street in the city centre of London (probably Regent Street).

The street is filled with cars, taxis (the famous London black cabs) and red double-decker buses and the traffic is very heavy. There are also pedestrians crossing from one side to the other and, in the middle of the street, a row of street lamps. On both sides, and especially on the right, we can see a lot of different buildings and shops and, in front of them, many people walking on the pavement.

In the background, we can notice beautiful white buildings at the top of which some flags are slightly flying in a clear blue sky.

À TON TOUR !

Complète la description de cette photo de Londres en utilisant le vocabulaire de la fiche.

London bus and cab,
Bjørn Hovdal

This photograph was .... by Bjørn Hovdal, a Norwegian photographer. It is simply .... "London bus and cab" but it .... more than just a bus and a taxi: it is a typical view of Westminster and Big Ben.

The picture is in .... except for the red double-decker bus. In the ...., we can see a black cab in the .... and two police officers on horses on the ....

In the ...., there are the Houses of Parliament and London's famous clock tower: Big Ben.

CORRIGÉ p.104 D'AUTRES EXERCICES : fiche 21

EXPRESSION ÉCRITE

Raconter un souvenir d'enfance

17

Pour raconter un souvenir, tu dois savoir situer les événements dans le passé et en indiquer la chronologie. Tu utilises les temps du passé, principalement le prétérit.

LA BOÎTE À OUTILS

1 Introduire et organiser le récit

« Distingue les différentes étapes de ton récit en faisant plusieurs paragraphes. »

▶ Pour commencer, **situe ton récit** dans le passé.

When I was 5... *Quand j'avais 5 ans...*
last year / last summer: *l'année dernière / l'été dernier*
a long time ago / four years ago: *il y a longtemps / il y a quatre ans*

▶ Utilise des **marqueurs temporels** pour indiquer la chronologie des événements.

at first, in the beginning: *d'abord, au début* • then: *alors, ensuite*
a few minutes later: *quelques minutes plus tard*
while...: *pendant que...* • in the meantime: *pendant ce temps-là*
at/in the end, finally: *enfin, finalement, à la fin*

2 Utiliser les temps du passé de façon judicieuse

▶ Le temps de base du récit au passé est le **prétérit simple** (→ FICHE 28).

One summer, when I was a child, something amazing happened to me.

▶ Pour décrire les circonstances d'un événement, tu utilises le **prétérit *be + -ing***, qui équivaut le plus souvent à un imparfait en français.

They were driving (when they saw a bear).
Ils conduisaient (quand ils ont vu un ours).

▶ Pour évoquer un état révolu, une situation qui n'existe plus, tu emploies ***used to* + BV**.

I used to be very shy. *J'étais très timide (autrefois).*
I didn't use to have a cell phone. *Je n'avais pas de téléphone portable (avant).*

MOTS UTILES

Raconter une fête, une tradition

- to celebrate: *célébrer, fêter*
- a costume: *un déguisement*
- a bank/public holiday: *un jour férié*
- a present, a gift: *un cadeau*
- holidays/vacation [US]: *les vacances*
- the National Day: *la fête nationale*
- a festival: *une fête, un festival*
- Christmas, Xmas: *Noël*
- a party: *une fête, une soirée*
- Father Christmas / Santa Claus: *le Père Noël*

METTRE EN PRATIQUE

Write about a childhood memory

Sally raconte son meilleur souvenir de Noël.

I will never forget the first Christmas I spent at my grandparents' in the Alps when I was 6. It was on Xmas Eve and it was snowing... which was perfect!

I was determined to stay up all night to see Father Christmas. So I sat on the sofa and waited. Some time later, I was sleeping soundly when my mother woke me up.

"I heard something at the door", she said, "you should go and see".
I ran to the door, opened it and there I saw... Father Christmas! He left presents at his feet, wished me a Merry Christmas and disappeared in the dark. It was magical!

A few minutes later, while I was playing with my new robot, Grandpa joined me and I suddenly realized that something was different, something about his beard... It was big and white, like Father Xmas's beard. When I tried to touch it, it fell off!

That's how I knew that Father Xmas didn't exist...

À TON TOUR !

Rétablis les expressions et marqueurs temporels suivants dans ce récit d'un Noël passé en Australie.

At the time • on Christmas Day • After opening our presents • when I was 10 • While we were playing • 24 hours later • on December 23rd.

I remember the Christmas I spent in Australia ...., my uncle used to live in Sydney; so it was a great opportunity to spend Christmas in the sun. We took the plane from Paris .... and arrived in Sydney ...., on December 24th. After a good night's sleep, when I woke up ...., the sun was shining and there were presents everywhere in the garden! ...., my cousins and I played with our new toys for hours. ...., my parents and uncle were preparing everything to have a BBQ party on the beach. I had a wonderful time, and I'll never forget the only Xmas I spent in my swimming shorts!

CORRIGÉ p.104 D'AUTRES EXERCICES : fiche 21

Rédiger le portrait de quelqu'un

18

Quand tu présentes quelqu'un, tu peux décrire son physique mais aussi sa personnalité. Tu dois savoir formuler une description précise et nuancée.

LA BOÎTE À OUTILS

1 Présenter quelqu'un et exprimer son avis

▶ Commence par **introduire** ce dont tu vas parler.

I'd like to introduce / to describe… *J'aimerais présenter/décrire…*

▶ Sers-toi du **présent simple** pour exprimer ton point de vue (le présent en *be* + V-*ing* ne s'utilise que pour décrire une action en cours).

▶ Utilise des **verbes** pour dire ce que tu penses ou ce que tu ressens.

I think, I believe, I feel, I admit (that)… [opinion]
I love, I like, I envy, I hate, I can't bear, I don't mind… [sentiments]

2 Faire une description nuancée

▶ Lorsque tu décris quelqu'un, tu utilises des **adjectifs** qui permettent à ton lecteur de se représenter la personne que tu évoques.

▶ N'emploie pas toujours *be* pour introduire les adjectifs.

He ~~is~~ shy → He looks/seems shy. / I find him shy…

▶ Utilise des **adverbes** pour nuancer le sens des adjectifs.

a bit, quite, very, extremely… (+ adj.) : *un peu, assez, très, extrêmement…*

▶ Emploie aussi des comparatifs ou des superlatifs. (→ FICHE 25).

- as tall as…: *aussi grand que…*
- the same as…: *le même que…*
- taller than: *plus grand que*
- more/less intelligent than: *plus/moins intelligent que…*

« Pour dire "moins… que", tu peux aussi utiliser *not as… as…* »

MOTS UTILES

Décrire la personnalité de quelqu'un

- nice, kind: *gentil(le)*
- mean, nasty: *méchant(-e)*
- generous: *généreux(-se)*
- selfish: *égoïste*
- boring: *ennuyeux(-se)*
- hardworking: *travailleur*
- lazy: *paresseux(-se)*
- easy-going: *facile à vivre*
- clumsy: *maladroit(e)*
- absent-minded: *étourdi(e), distrait(e)*

METTRE EN PRATIQUE

Describe your best friend

Jenna décrit son meilleur ami, Sebastian.

I'd like to introduce my best friend Sebastian. Sebby (as I call him) and I have a lot in common: he is thirteen, just like me, he is as tall as me, goes to the same school and plays the same sports as me. So, I see him almost every day... and I love it!

I really like him because he is very nice, extremely generous and he's always ready to help when someone is in trouble. He looks quite shy, but I find him funny and easy-going. That's why I enjoy spending time with him.

I have to admit that he isn't perfect... but who is?? His parents say that he can sometimes be a bit clumsy, that he is not as patient as I am and that he's the most absent-minded boy in the world... The truth is I really don't care what they say because Sebby is my best friend and I like him just the way he is!

À TON TOUR !

1 Complète cette présentation en entourant les verbes qui conviennent.

I don't make / doesn't make / make friends easily, so I have / haven't got / has got only one close friend. Her name am / has / is Lisa and she live / lives / don't live in Paris, just like me.

We go / goes / doesn't go to the same school and we has / have / don't have the same tastes: we both likes / like / doesn't like playing tennis and reading fantasy books but we likes / like / don't like listening to rap music.

I know Lisa isn't / is / are always perfect: she can sometimes be a bit lazy and jealous , but I care / don't care / doesn't care because she is the nicest person I don't know / knows / know and the best friend in the world!

Attention à la conjugaison du présent simple : pense au -s final à la 3e personne du singulier (→ FICHE 27).

2 Trouve le contraire des adjectifs suivants.

1. lazy ≠ ....

2. stupid ≠ ....

3. nice ≠ ....

4. selfish ≠ ....

CORRIGÉ p.105 D'AUTRES EXERCICES : fiche 21

EXPRESSION ÉCRITE

Argumenter sur un thème

19

Pour rédiger une argumentation efficace, tu dois savoir organiser tes idées mais aussi justifier ton point de vue.

LA BOÎTE À OUTILS

1 Exposer son opinion

▶ Avant de donner ton opinion, introduis le **thème** que tu vas aborder.

People usually say/think... *On dit/pense souvent...*
We may wonder / We can ask ourselves if... *On peut se demander si...*

▶ Indique clairement que tu exprimes une **opinion personnelle**.

I think/believe (that)... *Je pense/crois que...*
in my opinion / to my mind: *à mon avis*
as far as I'm concerned: *en ce qui me concerne*

2 Exprimer un avis nuancé

▶ **Organise tes arguments** de façon logique et cohérente.

first: *d'abord* • then: *puis, ensuite* • finally: *enfin*
what's more / furthermore: *de plus*
that's why: *c'est pourquoi*
indeed: *en effet* • actually, in fact: *en fait*
in conclusion / to conclude: *en conclusion*

« Tu peux donner des exemples issus de ton expérience personnelle. »

▶ **Illustre ton point de vue** par des exemples.

for example, for instance: *par exemple*

▶ Tu peux aussi **réagir** à l'opinion d'autres personnes.

I agree / I don't agree with you.
Je suis d'accord / Je ne suis pas d'accord avec toi.

MOTS UTILES

Argumenter sur les nouvelles technologies

- a computer: *un ordinateur*
- a laptop: *un ordinateur portable*
- a screen: *un écran*
- a mobile (phone) [UK] / a cell(ular) phone [US]: *un téléphone portable*
- to be addicted to: *être accro à*
- to text sb: *envoyer un SMS à qqn*
- to surf the Internet: *naviguer sur Internet*
- to google sth: *chercher qch sur Google*
- a social network: *un réseau social*

METTRE EN PRATIQUE

New technologies

Alicia doit répondre au sujet suivant : *Do you think new technologies can be dangerous for children and teenagers?*

We, teenagers, were born with computers and the Internet. But nowadays people usually say we spend too much time on screens, on our phones or tablets – which is supposed to be bad for us. So, we can ask ourselves if new technologies are not taking too much space in our lives.

As far as I'm concerned, I always have my mobile phone with me and I like spending some time on Facebook but I don't agree with people who think all teenagers are computer addicts.

Indeed, I think new technologies are good for all of us. For instance, I use the Internet a lot for my school work: it is an incredible source of information.

Furthermore, new technologies keep me connected with my friends and family all the time. If my mother worries about me, she can phone or text me and know immediately where I am. That's why I believe new technologies make our world easier and safer.

To conclude, I feel that using technology is not more dangerous for teenagers than riding a bike on the road. We just have to know how to use it safely.

À TON TOUR !

Un autre élève de la classe a répondu au même sujet mais a fait quelques erreurs, rayées sur la copie. Aide-le à faire les corrections nécessaires.

~~At the past~~ ...., when my grandparents were young ~~by example~~ ...., people didn't have any computers and still, most children were happy. So we can ~~ask us~~ .... why children can't even imagine living without a smart phone or a tablet ~~in our days~~ ....

I'm a teenager myself, but I ~~am agree~~ .... with the people who say that young people spend too much time on screens.

My brother is the best (or worst!) ~~exemple~~ .... I have. ~~In effect~~ ...., he spends his time playing on his tablet all day!

To tell the truth, I worry about him and children in general: ~~to my opinion~~ .... new technology can change them into antisocial beings or even zombies. ~~It is for why~~ .... I think parents should be very careful.

CORRIGÉ p.105
D'AUTRES EXERCICES : fiche 21

EXPRESSION ÉCRITE

Rédiger un courriel

20

Comme en français, la rédaction d'un courrier (lettre ou courriel) en anglais obéit à certaines règles : tu dois notamment savoir l'introduire et le terminer.

LA BOÎTE À OUTILS

1 Introduire un courriel

▶ Commencer ton courrier par ***Dear*** ou ***Hello/Hi*** (informel).

Dear Sir or Madam, Dear Mrs/Mr Smith, Dear Jane...

▶ Démarre le **corps du message** en expliquant ce qui motive ton courriel.

- Many thanks for your mail.
  Merci beaucoup pour votre mail.
- I'm writing to tell/ask you...
  Je vous écris pour vous dire / demander...
- In reply to your message...
  En réponse à votre message...

« N'oublie pas de renseigner l'objet du mail (*subject*). »

2 Terminer le courrier

▶ **Conclus** en invitant ton destinataire à te répondre.

- I should be grateful if you could (+ BV)...
  Je vous serais reconnaissant(e) de (+ inf.)...
- I'm looking forward to hearing from you.
  J'attends de vos nouvelles avec impatience.
- Write soon! *Écris-moi vite !*

▶ Choisis enfin une **formule de clôture** adaptée à ton destinataire.

Yours truly / Yours sincerely: *Mes sincères salutations*
Best wishes / Kind regards: *Amicalement*
See you soon: *À bientôt*
(Lots of) love: *(Gros) bisous*

MOTS UTILES

Proposer des activités sportives

- to do sports (judo, gymnastics): *faire du sport (du judo, de la gym...)*
- to play (football, tennis...): *jouer (au football, au tennis...)*
- to go + V-ing: *aller faire (une activité)*
- canoeing: *le canoë*
- climbing: *l'escalade*
- hiking, trekking, walking: *la randonnée*
- horse riding: *l'équitation*
- mountain biking: *le VTT*
- sailing: *la voile*
- scuba diving: *la plongée*
- swimming: *la natation*

METTRE EN PRATIQUE

Write an email to a friend

Alex écrit un courriel à un ami Ethan pour l'inviter pour le week-end.

From: alex.hill@coldmail.co.uk
To: ethan.forg@jmail.com
Subject: this weekend ☺

Hi, Ethan!

Many thanks for your last email. It was great to hear from you.
I hope you are fine and your new school is ok. Have you made some friends yet? Well, of course, you will never meet anyone as perfect as I am... but you can try! ;)

I must admit that I found it hard, this year, to go back to school without my best friend... That's why I'm writing to tell you I got a brilliant idea: how about coming over for the weekend? Mum is alright with that.

I thought we could go hiking or mountain biking. I suggest we go for a hike on Saturday and we spend Sunday afternoon at Blue Lake with my family. We could go canoeing or sailing. What do you think?

I'm looking forward to your answer! And say hello to your family ☺
Alex

À TON TOUR !

Ethan répond à son ami pour accepter son invitation et lui indiquer les activités qui l'intéressent ou non. Rédige sa réponse en t'aidant des illustrations suivantes.

....

....

....

....

....

Ethan commence par remercier Alex, puis il lui indique ce qu'il veut faire ou ne pas faire. Enfin, il conclut avec enthousiasme et signe.

CORRIGÉ p.105 D'AUTRES EXERCICES : fiche 21

Quiz express

Vérifie que tu as retenu les points clés des fiches 16 à 20

21

Réponds à chacun des quiz, puis résous l'énigme.

Expression écrite

1 Décrire une image

Fiche 16

Relie les éléments des deux colonnes pour former une expression correcte, puis associe-la au numéro correspondant sur le schéma.

	• the top: ....
in •	• the bottom: ....
on •	• the middle: ....
at •	• the left ....
	• the right ....
	• the top right-hand corner ....

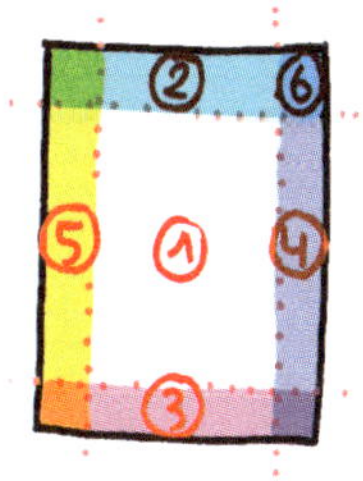

2 Raconter un souvenir d'enfance

Fiche 17

Remets ce récit dans l'ordre en numérotant les phrases de 1 à 8 (aide-toi de la ponctuation et des expressions de temps).

...... **a.** We saw many wonderful sights during our stay,
...... **b.** I remember we landed at Heathrow Airport at 11 a.m
...... **c.** and then, after a quick lunch, we started visiting the city.
...... **d.** and, a few minutes later, we were on a bus to the city centre.
...... **e.** Three years ago, we went to London for a week in the summer.
...... **f.** we saw Big Ben from the top of the London Eye... and I loved it!
...... **g.** First, we went to our hotel to leave our luggage
...... **h.** but I'll never forget what we did on the last day:

3 Rédiger le portrait de quelqu'un

Fiche 18

Associe correctement les éléments des deux colonnes.

1. My brother Alex is 3 years older •	• playing the guitar.
2. He loves •	• playing tennis together.
3. He doesn't like the same things •	• than me.
4. But we like •	• as me.
5. I think he is the laziest person •	• in the world.
6. But he is also the nicest brother •	• in the family.

4 Argumenter sur un thème

Entoure l'équivalent le plus proche des expressions proposées.

1. We may wonder: we can ask ourselves • we can answer • we argue
2. To believe: to argue • to think • to understand
3. As far as I'm concerned: in my opinion • about me • I'm very worried
4. Furthermore: however • nevertheless • in addition
5. Actually: in fact • nowadays • indeed
6. For instance: on the contrary • for example • to insist

5 Écrire un courriel

Tu écris un email à ta meilleure amie. Raye à chaque fois deux formules ou expressions qu'il est peu probable que tu utilises.

1. a. Dear Sir b. Dear Madam c. Dear Abby d. Hi, Abby!
2. a. I'm writing to tell you... b. I'd like to tell you... c. I am honoured to write to you... d. In reply to your letter, I would like to...
3. a. I am looking forward to your answer. b. I am looking forward to hearing from you. c. Please, write soon! d. Let me know asap!
4. a. Yours truly b. Yours sincerely c. See you soon d. Love

ÉNIGME

Cherche la traduction des mots suivants en anglais, puis trouve-les dans la grille, horizontalement ou verticalement. Avec les lettres restantes remises dans l'ordre, tu trouveras le mot mystère.

dessin • dessin humoristique • affiche • pub • tableau • couverture

C	A	R	T	O	O	N	P	I
O	P	A	I	N	T	I	N	G
V	C	A	D	V	E	R	T	T
E	U	G	N	I	W	A	R	D
R	R	R	E	T	S	O	P	E

Mot mystère : _ _ _ _ _ _ _

drawing : cartoon : poster : advert : painting : cover.
Le mot mystère est : *picture* (image).

Reporte-toi aux corrigés p. 105-106 et calcule ton score. **Score : .../23**

Le nom

En anglais, les noms ne sont pas nécessairement précédés d'un article. Ils ont le plus souvent un pluriel en -s, mais il existe des pluriels irréguliers qu'il faut connaître.

L'ESSENTIEL

1 Les articles

▶ Pour dire « un » ou « une », on emploie l'article ***a*** devant un son de consonne et ***an*** devant un son de voyelle.

a dog, an animal • a teacher, an English teacher • a horror movie, an hour [le *h* de *hour* ne se prononce pas]

▶ On utilise ***the*** pour dire « le, la, les » quand on parle de quelqu'un ou de quelque chose de particulier, que l'on pourrait désigner ou qui est clairement identifié.

Look at the girl over there. [celle qui est là-bas]
The bus is late again! [celui que nous prenons]

▶ En revanche, pour parler d'une généralité, on emploie l'article zéro (Ø), c'est-à-dire qu'il n'y a **pas d'article** devant le nom.

I like Ø chocolate. • Ø Teenagers are very interested in Ø new technologies.

2 Le pluriel des noms

▶ Le **pluriel régulier** se forme simplement en ajoutant *-s* au nom.
Si le nom se termine par *-s*, *-x*, *-ch*, *-sh* ou *-o*, on ajoute *-es*.
Si le nom se termine par une consonne +*y*, on remplace le *-y* par *-ies*.

a book, two books • a tomato, three tomatoes • a city, four cities

▶ Certains **pluriels** courants sont **irréguliers**… et à apprendre !

a man → two men • a woman → two women • a child → two children
a foot → two feet • a tooth → two teeth • a mouse → two mice

À RETENIR

La terminaison -s ou *-es* du pluriel se prononce…

- /s/ après les sons /f/, /k/, /p/, /t/ → *caps, hats*
- /ɪz/ après les sons /s/, /z/, /ʃ/, /dʒ/ → *glasses, messages*
- /z/ dans les autres cas → *pupils, ideas*

À TON TOUR !

1 Complète les phrases suivantes avec *a(n)* ou *the*.

1. I've got two pets, ... cat and .... hamster.
2. Look at .... woman crossing .... street: she's my French teacher!
3. I've got .... idea! Meet me in .... hour in front of .... school.
4. My grandparents have got .... house in Scotland.

2 Complète les phrases suivantes avec *the* ou Ø.

1. Do you remember .... name of .... main actor in Twilight?
2. I usually love .... animals, but I hate .... dog that my sister got for her birthday. He always barks at .... people who are with her! [to bark: *aboyer*]
3. I don't like .... coffee, I prefer .... tea.
4. .... English is a beautiful language

3 Complète la grille avec le pluriel des mots proposés, puis donne le singulier du mot mystère qui apparaîtra dans les cases colorées.

CHILD
BUS
PUPPY
BOY
MOUSE
FOOT
TOOTH
ROSE
REWARD

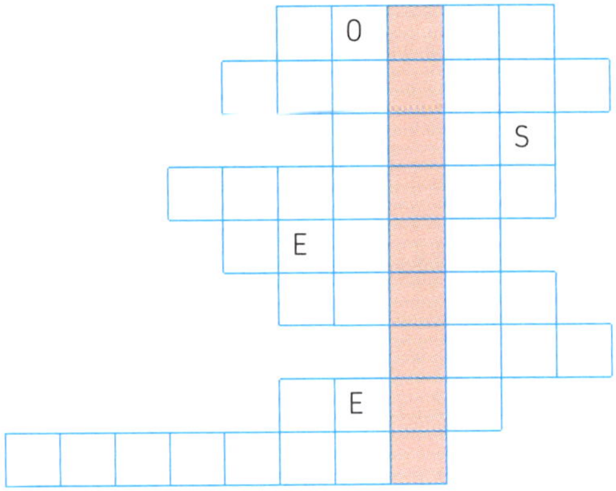

Mot mystère : a _ _ _ _ _ _ _ _ _

4 Prononce ces mots au pluriel puis classe-les dans le tableau en fonction de la prononciation de leur terminaison.

pages • potatoes • girls • presents • cats • watches

/s/	/iz/	/z/

CORRIGÉ p.106

D'AUTRES EXERCICES : fiche 26

Les quantifieurs

Quand on veut parler d'une certaine quantité ou d'un certain nombre sans le préciser, on utilise des quantifieurs.

L'ESSENTIEL

1 Parler d'une grande ou d'une petite quantité

Le **choix du quantifieur** dépend de la quantité que tu veux exprimer et du nombre du nom qui suit (singulier ou pluriel).

quantité exprimée	nom pluriel	nom singulier
Grande quantité : *beaucoup (de)*	many a lot of, lots of	much a lot of, lots of
Quantité insuffisante : *peu (de)*	few	little
Petite quantité : quelques, *un peu (de)*	a few	a little

There is **a lot of** traffic tonight.
"Did you take **many** photos?" "No, I took very **few**".
He hasn't got **much** money: he has **little** money.
I have **a few** close friends. • There is only **a little** milk left.

ASTUCE

A lot of et *lots of* s'utilisent avec n'importe quel nom, contrairement à *much* et *many*. Si tu hésites pour traduire « beaucoup de », emploie *a lot of* : tu es sûr(e) de ne pas te tromper !

2 Parler d'une certaine quantité

▶ *Some*, *any* et *no* servent à exprimer une **quantité indéfinie** et s'utilisent devant des noms au singulier ou au pluriel. Ils se traduisent le plus souvent par « du, de la, des ».

▶ ***Some*** s'emploie surtout dans les phrases affirmatives, mais aussi dans les questions lorsque l'on offre quelque chose.

I'd like **some** water, please. • Would you like **some** tea?

▶ ***Any*** s'utilise dans les autres phrases interrogatives.

Is there **any** cheddar cheese in the fridge?

▶ À la **forme négative**, on utilise *not… any* + nom ou *no* + nom.

There is**n't any** bread left = There is **no** bread left. *Il ne reste pas de pain.*

À TON TOUR !

1 Réécris les phrases en remplaçant *a lot of* par *much* ou *many*.

1. Did you have a lot of problems there?

....

2. Sorry, I'm busy. I don't have a lot of time to talk to you.

....

3. I'm lucky, there aren't a lot of pupils in my class this year.

....

4. She doesn't want to eat a lot (of food). She doesn't feel very well.

....

2 Complète les phrases suivantes avec *few* ou *little* selon le cas.

1. It was so cold that there were very .... people in the street.
2. There's too .... chocolate left. We can't make cookies!
3. She is very shy, she's got .... friends.
4. .... students study Korean at university.
5. I'm sad to see he's making so .... progress.

3 Barre dans chaque phrase les propositions qui ne conviennent pas.

1. You shouldn't drink so little / few / much coffee! Or you won't sleep tonight...
2. There aren't many / few / some visitors today, we can stay in the park as long as we like.
3. I'd like to make some / any / a brownies. I need a few / no / some butter. Have you got some / any / little?

4 Reformule ces phrases en utilisant *not... any*.

1. My friends have no pets.

....

2. There's no solution yet.

....

3. I have no clue how to solve the problem.

....

4. He had no money at the time.

....

Any n'est pas un mot négatif. Pense à mettre le verbe à la forme négative et fais attention au temps !

CORRIGÉ p.107 D'AUTRES EXERCICES : fiche 26

La possession

24

Pour parler de ce que l'on possède, **have (got)** *n'est pas la seule solution : on peut utiliser des adjectifs et des pronoms possessifs ou encore le génitif.*

L'ESSENTIEL

1 Les adjectifs et pronoms possessifs

pronom personnel sujet	adjectif possessif	pronom possessif
I	my	mine
he / she /it	his / her /its	his / hers / its
we	our	ours
you	your	yours
they	their	theirs

This is my book, not yours! • I know his name, but I don't know hers.

▶ Il n'y a qu'un seul adjectif et pronom possessif par personne en anglais, alors qu'il en existe plusieurs en français : *my* peut se traduire « ma, mon, mes » et *mine* par « le mien, la mienne, les miens, les miennes ».

▶ En anglais, le possessif **s'accorde avec le possesseur**.

his ball (his) • her ball (hers) • its ball (its)

ASTUCE

Les adjectifs et pronoms possessifs se ressemblent, mais l'adjectif possessif est un déterminant : il est toujours suivi d'un groupe nominal.

2 Le génitif ('s ou ')

▶ Le génitif sert aussi à exprimer la possession : il se place donc avant le groupe nominal (comme le déterminant possessif). Mais l'ordre des mots est l'inverse du français : **possesseur + *'s* + objet possédé.**

Tom's bag (his bag) — le sac de Tom

Emma's phone (her phone) — le téléphone d'Emma

▶ Après un nom pluriel en *-s*, on n'ajoute que **l'apostrophe (sans *s*)**.

my parents' car, *mais* : the children's toys [pluriel irrégulier]

À TON TOUR !

1 **Complète les phrases par l'adjectif possessif qui convient (aide-toi du sujet souligné).**

1. Tony is on holiday with .... family.

2. Tony and his family are spending a few days in .... house in Spain.

3. We visited that museum with .... class last year.

4. Are you coming to the party with .... sister?

2 **Remets un peu d'ordre… Relie chaque objet à son propriétaire à l'aide du texte ci-dessous.**

This is her cap but that's his hat. These jeans are his, but those shorts are hers. The roses are hers but the blue flowers aren't, they must be its flowers. And look at that! Is it a belt or a collar? It must be a collar, it must be its.

3 **Reformule les phrases en remplaçant le déterminant possessif par un génitif (avec le nom entre parenthèses).**

1. Her bag is too heavy for her. (*Emily*)

....

2. His computer is broken! (*James*)

....

3. Their house has been burgled. (*My neighbours*) [to burgle: *cambrioler*]

....

4. I can't find their ball! (*the children*)

....

CORRIGÉ p.107 D'AUTRES EXERCICES : fiche 26

Comparatifs et superlatifs

25

On utilise les comparatifs quand on compare deux éléments et les superlatifs quand on compare plus de deux éléments.

L'ESSENTIEL

1 Les comparatifs

▶ Le comparatif de **supériorité** (« plus… que ») se forme différemment en fonction de la longueur de l'adjectif.

Adj. d'une syll.	adj. + -er + *than*	I'm older than you.
Adj. longs	*more* + adj. + *than*	She's more intelligent than him.

▶ Le comparatif d'**égalité** (« aussi… que ») se construit avec *as* + adj. + *as*.

Alex is as tall as his father now.

▶ Le comparatif d'**infériorité** (« moins… que ») se forme avec *less* + adj. + *than* ou *not as* + adj. + *as* (surtout avec les adj. courts).

My new phone is less complicated than the old one.
Your dog is not as cute as mine.

2 Les superlatifs

Le superlatif de **supériorité** (« le plus… »), comme le comparatif, se forme différemment selon la longueur de l'adjectif.

Adj. d'une syll.	*the* + adj. + *-est*	I'm the oldest pupil in the class.
Adj. longs	*the most* + adj.	She's the most intelligent girl I know.

3 Les irréguliers

Adjectif	Comparatif de sup.	Superlatif de sup.
good/well (*bon/bien*)	better	the best
bad (*mauvais/mal*)	worse	the worst
far (*loin*)	farther/further	the farthest/the furthest

ATTENTION

- Adjectif de deux syllabes en *-y* : on remplace le *y* par *-ier* ou *-iest*.
  happy → happier, the happiest
- Adjectif en consonne-voyelle-consonne : on double la consonne.
  big → bigger, the biggest

À TON TOUR !

1 Complète les phrases suivantes en mettant l'adjectif entre parenthèses au comparatif d'égalité (=), d'infériorité (-) ou de supériorité (+).

1. Her brother is .... (*old* +) her but he is .... (*tall* =) her and he looks .... (*childish* +). [childish: *enfantin, puéril*]

2. I think exercise 1 is .... (*difficult* +) exercise 3 and it is .... (*amusing* -)!

3. I am .... (*good* +) at English .... at Spanish, but I'm .... (*good* =) at Math .... at Physics.

> *As* et *than* se traduisent tous deux par « que » en français, mais ne s'emploient pas avec les mêmes comparatifs.

2 Mets l'adjectif entre parenthèses au superlatif de supériorité.

1. New York is .... (*large*) and .... (*expensive*) city in the USA.

2. The Lut desert in Iran is probably .... (*hot*) place on Earth.

3. What is .... (*easy*) and .... (*comfortable*) way to travel between Paris and London?

3 Dans la grille ci-dessous, retrouve horizontalement, verticalement ou en diagonale les comparatifs et superlatifs des adjectifs de la liste. Avec les lettres restantes, tu pourras écrire un autre superlatif.

Comparatifs de supériorité de : BIG • GOOD • NICE • SAFE • FAR • HAPPY • SAD.

Superlatifs de supériorité (sans *the*) de : BAD • GOOD • TALL • FAR • SLIM • WELL.

B	I	G	G	E	R	R	B	S
T	H	A	P	P	I	E	R	L
S	S	W	O	R	S	T	E	I
E	A	E	U	T	N	T	H	M
L	F	D	B	G	I	E	T	M
L	E	L	D	I	C	B	R	E
A	R	E	S	E	E	T	A	S
T	S	E	H	T	R	U	F	T

Superlatif caché : _ _ _ _ _ _ _ _ , de l'adjectif ....

CORRIGÉ p.107 D'AUTRES EXERCICES : fiche 26

Quiz express

Vérifie que tu as retenu les points clés des ▸ fiches 22 à 25

26

Réponds à chacun des quiz, puis résous l'énigme.

Le groupe nominal

1 Le pluriel des noms

Fiche 22

Quelles lettres manquent pour mettre ces noms au pluriel ?
Relie les noms et leur terminaison.

1. a potato → two potato... •
2. a pencil → two pencil... • • -s
3. a phone → two phone... • • -es
4. a woman → two wom... • • -ies
5. a party → two part... • • -en
6. a brush → two brush... •

2 Les articles : *a, an, the* ou Ø

Fiche 22

Entoure le déterminant qui convient.

1. Ø / The teachers we have this year are quite nice.
2. His mother is a / an English teacher.
3. The / Ø French people aren't very good at languages.
4. The / Ø pupils in my class are very good at English.

3 Les quantifieurs

Fiche 23

Coche le quantifieur qui convient dans les phrases suivantes.

1. There were so ☐ much ☐ many ☐ little people at the concert that I couldn't see you.
2. Hurry up, please! I don't have ☐ much ☐ many ☐ little time!
3. There's too ☐ little ☐ few ☐ much time left! I can't finish tonight.
4. I'd like to make ☐ a little ☐ a few ☐ any recommendations before I go.
5. Leave me alone! I don't need ☐ some ☐ any ☐ much help!
6. I'm sorry! There's ☐ some ☐ any ☐ no cake left.

4 La possession

Fiche 24

Raye la proposition incorrecte dans chacune des phrases.

1. Mr and Mrs Smith own this house: it's his house / their house / theirs.
2. I like Jane's jeans, but I don't like Tony's jeans: I prefer hers / his jeans / her jeans.
3. My sister's boyfriend looks like an actor. His boyfriend / Her boyfriend / he is so gorgeous!

5 Les comparatifs

Fiche 25

Relie les éléments des différentes colonnes pour construire trois phrases complètes.

Cars •	• are •	• as eco-friendly •	• than •	• bikes.
	• aren't •	• faster •	• as •	
		• more expensive •		

6 Les superlatifs

Fiche 25

Souligne dans le texte les six superlatifs de supériorité.

My father is older than my mother but he is more patient than her: he is the most patient person I know! My mother is very clever. I often tell her she's the most intelligent woman on earth! My older sister is the prettiest girl in the family. She is very nice, but not as nice as my brother Tim. Tim is the nicest boy and the best brother in the world! As for me, maybe I'm not the most wonderful daughter and sister you can dream of, but I know I'm lucky to have such a great family!

ÉNIGME

Déchiffre cette citation attribuée à l'écrivain américain Mark Twain : utilise le code, puis devine les lettres manquantes.

♋ = A ♌ = B ♏ = E ♑ = G ☟ = H ♓ = I
& = K ● = L ○ = M □ = O ❒ = R ◆ = U

☟◆○□❒ ♓• ○♋■&♓■♎'• ♑❒♏♋◆♏•◆

HUMOR IS MANKIND'S GREATEST

♌●♏• •♓■♑.

BLESSING

Humor is mankind's greatest blessing.

Reporte-toi aux corrigés p. 108 et calcule ton score.

Score : .../19

Le présent

27

En anglais, il existe deux présents : le présent simple pour parler d'actions habituelles ou régulières et le présent be + V-ing pour parler d'actions en cours.

L'ESSENTIEL

1 Le présent simple

▶ On utilise le présent simple pour parler de goûts, d'habitudes, de **faits réguliers ou permanents**.

▶ Sa conjugaison n'a que **deux formes**, une pour la 3e personne du singulier et une pour les autres personnes. Aux formes négative et interrogative, on utilise l'auxiliaire *do* (*does* à la 3e personne du singulier).

	I / we / you / they	he / she / it
Forme affirmative	I play	She plays
Forme négative	We dont' (do not) play	He doesn't (does not) play
Forme interrogative	Do you play?	Does she play?

▶ Avec le présent simple, l'**adverbe de fréquence** est placé avant le verbe.

I always get up at 7 a.m. • I don't often walk to school.

2 Le présent en *be* + V-*ing*

▶ On utilise le présent *be* + V-*ing* pour parler d'**actions en cours** au moment où l'on parle ou d'actions à venir.

They are crying. [action en cours] • I'm going out tonight. [action à venir]

▶ Pour le former, on conjugue ***be* au présent simple** suivi du verbe qui indique l'action avec la terminaison *-ing*.

	I	he / she / it	we / you / they
Forme affirm.	I'm (am) playing.	She's (is) playing.	We are playing
Forme nég.	I'm not (am not) playing.	He isn't (is not) playing.	They aren't (are not) playing.
Forme interr.	Am I playing?	Is she playing?	Are you playing?

ASTUCE

Les verbes qui expriment un goût ou une opinion ne désignent pas des actions en cours : ils s'emploient donc généralement au présent simple.

I like English. • I think you're right!

À TON TOUR !

1 Que sont-ils en train de faire ? Écris une phrase au présent *be* + V-*ing* pour décrire chacune des illustrations.

1

2

3

4

1. ……………………………………………………………………
2. ……………………………………………………………………
3. ……………………………………………………………………
4. ……………………………………………………………………

Attention à l'orthographe des formes en -*ing* !

2 Remets ces mots dans l'ordre pour faire des phrases correctes au présent simple.

1. people / left / the / drive / England / always / in / on

……………………………………………………………………

2. ? / you / sometimes / go / do / Britain / to

……………………………………………………………………

3. often / tennis / brother / play / my / doesn't

……………………………………………………………………

3 Conjugue le verbe entre parenthèses au temps qui convient : présent simple ou présent *be* + V-*ing*.

1. I …………………………… (*not / think*) I can do it.
2. Be quiet, please! My brother and sister …………………………… (*sleep*)!
3. Listen! She …………………………… (*play*) the violin.
4. I love this picture, all my family …………………………… (*smile*).
5. He …………………… (*have*) football practice every Wednesday at 5 p.m.
6. Gary …………………………… (*not / like*) green beans very much.
7. We …………………………… (*have*) vegetable soup for dinner tonight.

CORRIGÉ p.109
D'AUTRES EXERCICES : fiche 32

LE VERBE

Le prétérit

28

Pour parler d'une action passée et révolue, on emploie le prétérit. Comme au présent, il existe une forme simple et une en be + V-ing.

L'ESSENTIEL

1 Le prétérit simple

▶ Le prétérit simple est le temps du passé le plus courant. On l'utilise pour parler d'**actions passées, complètement terminées**, sans lien avec le présent. On le traduit souvent par le passé composé.

I missed my bus this morning. *J'ai raté mon bus ce matin.*

▶ Des **marqueurs de temps** permettent de situer l'action dans le passé.

in 2016, last month, two weeks ago: ... *le mois dernier, il y a deux semaines*

▶ La conjugaison du prétérit est identique à toutes les personnes, sauf pour *be* qui a deux formes (*was* et *were*).

Forme affirmative	sujet + *V*-ed ou prétérit irrégulier (→ RABATS)
Forme négative	sujet + didn't + BV
Forme interrogative	Did + sujet + BV... ?

I worked • They didn't go • What did you do? • We ate [to eat, *v. irr.*]

2 Le prétérit en *be* + V-*ing*

On utilise le prétérit *be* + V-*ing* (ou prétérit continu) pour parler du déroulement d'une action dans le passé, ou pour **décrire les circonstances d'un événement passé**. On le traduit le plus souvent par un imparfait.

	I / he / she / it	we / you / they
Forme affirmative	*was* + V-*ing*	*were* + V-*ing*
Forme négative	*wasn't* + V-*ing*	*weren't* + V-*ing*
Forme interrogative	*Was* + sujet + V-*ing*... ?	*Were* + sujet + V-*ing*... ?

At 4 yesterday, I was playing, I wasn't working. What were you doing?
À 16 heures hier, j'étais en train de jouer, je ne travaillais pas. Que faisais-tu ?

À RETENIR

I was watching television when my mother arrived.

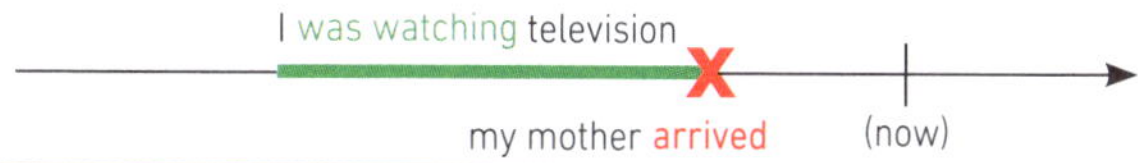

À TON TOUR !

1 Que vient-il de se passer ? Complète les phrases à l'aide des images ci-dessous. Emploie *just* et les verbes proposés au *present perfect*.

land • get married • miss • fall

1. The plane ....
2. She ....
3. The horse rider ....
4. They ....

Attention aux participes passés des verbes irréguliers (→ RABATS) !

2 Écris des phrases complètes à l'aide des mots suivants. Conjugue les verbes au *present perfect* à la personne qui convient.

1. My grandmother / in London / all her life / live.
....
2. My parents and I / be / to Paris / but / we / not / visit / the Eiffel Tower.
....
3. ? / you / read / J. K. Rowling's new book
....
4. What / do / she / again?
....

3 Complète avec *for* ou *since*.

1. .... five hours.
2. .... he was born.
3. .... April 14th.
4. .... many years.

4 Fais le bilan de tes expériences. Dis si tu as fait ou non ces actions.

play football • play baseball • paint • go to the USA • eat insects

....

....

....

....

CORRIGÉ p.110 D'AUTRES EXERCICES : fiche 32

Prétérit ou *present perfect* ?

30

Choisir entre le prétérit et le present perfect est souvent compliqué pour un francophone car tous deux peuvent traduire un passé composé.

L'ESSENTIEL

1 L'action a-t-elle un lien avec le présent ?

Pour choisir entre le prétérit et le *present perfect*, il ne faut pas se fier au français mais comprendre la valeur de chaque temps.

▶ Si l'action est **coupée du présent**, on utilise le prétérit.

I finished my homework this morning. Then, I went out.
Ce matin, j'ai fini mes devoirs. Puis je suis sorti.
[Chacune de ces actions est terminée : elles n'ont aucun lien avec le présent.]

▶ Si l'action est **en lien avec le présent**, qu'elle a des conséquences dans le présent, on emploie le *present perfect*.

I have finished my homework! I can go out now.
J'ai fini mes devoirs ! Maintenant je peux sortir.
[Ce qui importe ici, c'est le résultat de l'action sur le présent : je peux sortir.]

2 Repérer des indices

Certains mots peuvent te servir d'indices pour choisir le temps qui convient : les adverbes et mots interrogatifs qui évoquent un moment précis s'utilisent avec le prétérit ; ceux qui évoquent une durée, avec le *present perfect*.

Avec le prétérit	• When? How long ago? • ... ago [il y a...] last (+ *nom*) in (+ *année*), on (+ *date*)...	• When did you meet her? • I met her { two weeks ago. / last summer. / in 2015, on March 10th.
Avec le *present perfect*	• How long? • since... (→ FICHE 29) • always, never • ever/already [déjà] not... yet [pas encore]	• How long have you known her? I've known her since 2015. I've always known her. • Have you ever met her? No, I haven't met her yet.

NB : ***for*** n'a pas le même sens selon le temps avec lequel il est employé.

I worked at McDonald's for two years.
J'ai travaillé chez McDonald's pendant deux ans. [je n'y travaille plus]
I've worked at McDonald's for two years.
Je travaille chez McDonald's depuis deux ans. [j'y travaille toujours]

À TON TOUR !

1 Formule des questions et des réponses sur les expériences de Liam, comme dans l'exemple, en utilisant les éléments fournis.

> taste kangaroo meat • last year when in Australia
> "Have you ever tasted kangaroo meat?"
> "Yes, I tasted kangaroo meat last year when I was in Australia."

1. visit the Statue of Liberty • in August 2015

....

....

2. drive a sportscar • when in Le Mans last month

....

....

3. play the guitar at a school concert • never

....

....

Quand on évoque une action qui peut encore se produire, on utilise le *present perfect*, mais si l'on fait référence à une expérience particulière (dans le passé), on emploie le prétérit.

2 Associe les éléments pour former des phrases cohérentes.

1. How long ago... •
2. How long... •
3. I have never... •
4. Last night, I... •
5. We arrived here... •
6. We have lived here... •

• a. ... have you known her?
• b. ... did you meet her?
• c. ... since 2012.
• d. ... wrote a poem for you.
• e. ... written a poem.
• f. ... three years ago.

3 Conjugue les verbes au prétérit ou au *present perfect*.

1. My parents .... (*be*) to a lot of countries but they .... (*never / be*) to New Zealand.
2. My brother .... (*go*) to Iceland last year. He says it is the most beautiful place he .... (*ever / visit*).
3. This morning, I .... (*not / hear*) my alarm clock! Of course, I .... (*miss*) my bus , and I .... (*arrive*) late at school.
4. He .... (*play*) the piano since he was 5 and he .... (*always / be*) very good at it.

CORRIGÉ p.110 D'AUTRES EXERCICES : fiche 32

LE VERBE

Le passif

31

Contrairement au sujet d'une phrase active, le sujet de la phrase passive est… passif : ce n'est pas lui qui fait l'action, il la subit.

L'ESSENTIEL

1 Mettre une phrase au passif

▶ Pour mettre un verbe au passif, on conjugue ***be*** au temps et à la personne souhaités et on ajoute le **participe passé** du verbe en question.

Cricket is played in England, Australia, etc. [*be* au présent + p. passé de *play*]
All the brownies have been eaten. [*be* au present perfect + p. passé de *eat* (v. irr.)]

▶ Au passif, le sujet du verbe n'est pas celui qui fait l'action : c'est le **complément du verbe actif qui devient sujet**. Inversement, le sujet du verbe actif devient complément d'agent du verbe passif.

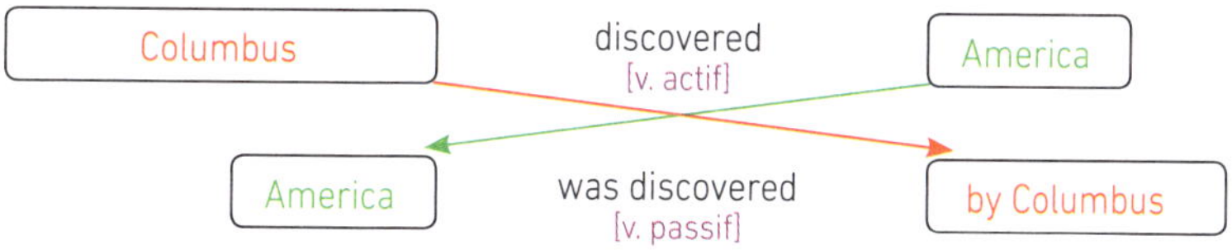

▶ Le **complément d'agent** est introduit par la préposition *by* (« par »).

Facebook was founded by Mark Zuckerberg.

On peut l'omettre lorsqu'il est évident ou qu'il n'a pas d'importance.

London was bombed during the Second World War.
[Inutile de préciser *by the Germans* : on sait que ce sont les Allemands qui ont bombardé.]
Dinner is served at 8 p.m. [Peu importe qui sert le dîner.]

2 Cas particulier : les verbes à deux compléments

Avec les verbes à deux compléments (*give*, *tell*, *buy*, *teach*…), il y a deux constructions passives possibles car chaque complément peut devenir sujet.

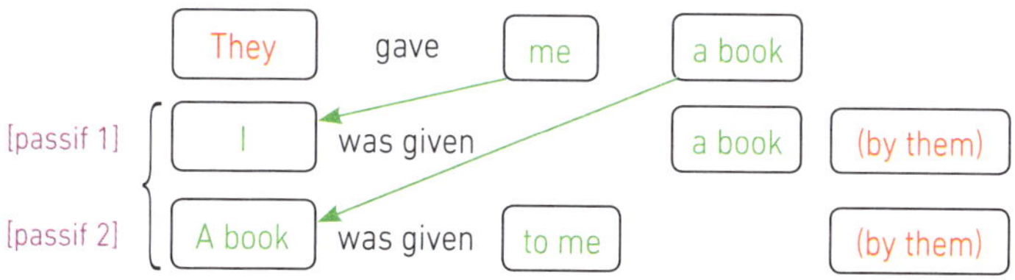

À TON TOUR !

1 Coche si ces phrases sont à l'actif ou au passif.

1. This won't be forgotten. ❑ actif ❑ passif
2. I have forgotten to tell you something. ❑ actif ❑ passif
3. She was very pretty when she was young. ❑ actif ❑ passif
4. She was offered a mobile phone for Christmas. ❑ actif ❑ passif
5. I am very good at drawing. ❑ actif ❑ passif

Un verbe au passif comporte toujours *be* + participe passé, et non pas seulement l'un ou l'autre.

2 Complète les phrases en fonction des illustrations, en mettant le verbe au prétérit, à la forme active ou passive.

❶ ride

❷ come home

❸ arrest

❹ give

1. This morning, Tony ....
2. When the rain started, Lana ....
3. One hour ago, the burglar ....
4. Yesterday, Bobby ....

3 Transforme ces phrases au passif en utilisant le complément souligné comme sujet. Ne mentionne le complément d'agent que si c'est utile.

1. They make <u>paper</u> from wood.

....

2. Our teachers give <u>us</u> a lot of homework.

....

3. He won't understand <u>that.</u>

....

4. Shakespeare wrote <u>*Hamlet* and *Romeo and Juliet*</u>.

....

Observe bien le temps de la phrase active et conjugue *be* au même temps au passif. Si le verbe à l'actif est précédé d'un modal, *be* sera précédé du même modal au passif.

CORRIGÉ p.111 D'AUTRES EXERCICES : fiche 32

Quiz express

Vérifie que tu as retenu les points clés des fiches 27 à 31

32

Réponds à chacun des quiz, puis résous l'énigme.

Le verbe (1)

1 Présent simple ou présent en *be* + V-*ing* ?

Fiche 27

Entoure la forme correcte.

1. I love / 'm loving going to the cinema.
2. Look at this picture! Everybody smiles / is smiling.
3. What do you do / are you doing now?
4. She doesn't work / isn't working today.
5. She doesn't usually work / isn't usually working on Wednesdays.

2 Le prétérit simple

Fiche 28

Raye, dans chaque liste, le verbe qui n'est pas conjugué au prétérit simple.

1. he played • he didn't play • he doesn't play • Did he play ?
2. we went • we didn't go • Did we go... ? • Do you go...?
3. she was • they have been • they were • they weren't
4. Have you seen...? • Did you see...? • I saw • I didn't see

3 Prétérit simple et prétérit *be* + V-*ing* ?

Fiche 28

Entoure la forme du verbe qui convient pour compléter les phrases suivantes.

1. He ran / was running / were running after the bus when I saw him.
2. They slept / was sleeping / were sleeping when I left home this morning.
3. We last played / was playing / were playing tennis together two years ago.
4. I made / was making / were making a cake when the bell rang.
5. When I arrived / was arriving / were arriving at the station, nobody was waiting for me.

4 Le *present perfect*

Fiche 29

Coche la traduction qui convient.

1. She has lived in the USA since 2012.

☐ a. Elle habite aux USA depuis 2012.

☐ b. Elle a habité aux USA en 2012.

2. How long have you worked here?

☐ a. Combien de temps as-tu travaillé ici?

☐ b. Depuis combien de temps travailles-tu ici?

3. I haven't seen him for more than a year.

Je ne l'ai pas vu ☐ a. depuis plus d'un an. ☐ b. pendant plus d'un an.

5 *Present perfect* ou prétérit ?

Fiche 30

Coche la forme du verbe qui convient.

1. I'm so happy I ☐ finished ☐ have finished my homework!
2. We ☐ were ☐ have been in Paris since Monday but we ☐ didn't visit ☐ haven't visited the Eiffel Tower yet.
3. They ☐ went ☐ have been to the Republic of Ireland in 2015 but they ☐ never went ☐ have never been to Northern Ireland.

6 Le passif

Fiche 31

Souligne dans le texte ci-dessous les quatre verbes au passif.

Slavery in America began when the first African slaves were brought to Virginia in 1619 and it was practiced almost everywhere in America in the 17th and 18th centuries. Slaves were owned by white masters and usually lived on farms or plantations under terrible conditions.

In the 19th century, a movement to abolish slavery grew in the North and divided the country. After the Civil War, millions of slaves were freed.

ÉNIGME

Remets ces anagrammes dans l'ordre pour reconstituer des participes passés. Attention, il y a des irréguliers !

S K A E D   N W I T E T R   P L E T S   D R E W O K   T G B H O U

_ _ _ _ _   _ _ _ _ _ _ _   _ _ _ _ _   _ _ _ _ _ _   _ _ _ _ _ _

asked • written • slept • worked • bought

Reporte-toi aux corrigés p. 111 et calcule ton score.

Score : .../24

Les modaux et leurs équivalents

33

Les modaux sont des auxiliaires qui permettent de nuancer le sens du verbe qu'ils accompagnent en lui donnant une valeur particulière (→ FICHE 34).

L'ESSENTIEL

1 Les caractéristiques des modaux

▶ Les modaux ont la **même forme** à toutes les personnes.

I must go to class now. • He must leave. • They must tell you the truth.
You can do anything. • She can play tennis very well. • We can sit here.

▶ Ils sont toujours suivis de la **base verbale**.

You must stay. • I may be late. • He can't speak French.

▶ Comme ce sont des **auxiliaires**, ils portent la négation et se placent devant le sujet dans les questions.

I can't (cannot) stay. • You mustn't (must not) do that.
Can you repeat, please? • May I come in?

2 Les équivalents

Il n'est pas possible de conjuguer un modal ou de l'utiliser avec un autre modal : on utilise donc des **expressions verbales** équivalentes qui, elles, peuvent se conjuguer ou s'utiliser après des modaux.

valeurs (→ FICHE 34)	modal	équivalent
capacité	can/could	be able to
incapacité	can't/couldn't [prét.]	not be able to, be unable to
permission	can/could, may	be allowed to
obligation	must	have to
interdiction	can't/couldn't, mustn't	not be allowed to, be forbidden to

- He could/was able to run faster when he was younger.
  Il pouvait courir plus vite quand il était plus jeune.
- I ~~didn't can~~ couldn't/wasn't allowed to have a mobile phone when I was in primary school.
  Je n'avais pas le droit d'avoir un téléphone portable quand j'étais en primaire.
- You ~~will must~~ will have to work harder if you want to have better grades.
  Tu devras travailler plus si tu veux avoir de meilleures notes.

À TON TOUR !

1 Un élève a fait de grosses erreurs dans ces phrases. Réécris une phrase correcte.

1. My brother can't ~~swimming~~ very well.

....

2. I ~~don't must~~ go out after 10 p.m.

....

3. ~~Do you can~~ help me?

....

4. They will ~~must~~ stay there.

....

2 Coche, pour chaque phrase contenant un modal, celle qui signifie la même chose.

1. I can't speak Spanish.
   ❑ I have to ❑ I'm not allowed to ❑ I'm not able to speak Spanish.
2. Can I open the window, please?
   ❑ Do I have to ❑ Am I able to ❑ Am I allowed to open the window?
3. You can't play ball in the classroom!
   ❑ You aren't able to ❑ You don't have to ❑ It's forbidden to play ball in the classroom!
4. They must be on time.
   ❑ They're able to ❑ They have to ❑ They're allowed to be on time.

Attention, *not have to* n'exprime pas l'interdiction mais l'absence d'obligation : « ne pas avoir à, ne pas être obligé de ».

3 Réécris ces phrases au prétérit en remplaçant les modaux par des expressions équivalentes.

1. I must go to the library to do some research on Charlotte Brontë.
   Yesterday, ...
2. He can't log onto his computer.
   This morning, he ....
3. We can sit down.
   The headmaster said ....
4. We mustn't park here.
   The policeman said ....
5. I can run for two hours without stopping.
   When I was young, ...

CORRIGÉ p.112 D'AUTRES EXERCICES : fiche 38

Les valeurs des modaux

34

Les modaux permettent d'exprimer la capacité, la permission, l'obligation, l'interdiction, la probabilité ou le conseil par exemple. Un même modal peut avoir différentes valeurs, en fonction du contexte.

L'ESSENTIEL

1 La capacité, la permission, l'obligation ou l'interdiction

▶ Pour exprimer la **capacité**, on utilise *can* au présent et *could* au passé. Leurs contraires *can't* (*cannot*) et *couldn't* expriment donc l'**incapacité**.

My little brother can swim now. *Mon petit frère sait nager maintenant.*
I could swim when I was 4. *Je savais nager quand j'avais 4 ans.*

▶ Pour exprimer la **permission**, dire ou demander ce que l'on peut faire, on peut employer *can* (*could* au passé) ou *may*.

- Mum says I can go to the cinema tonight.
  Maman dit que je peux aller au cinéma ce soir.
- May I speak to Jane?
  Puis-je parler à Jane ? [très poli]

▶ Pour exprimer l'**obligation**, dire ce que l'on doit faire, on emploie *must*.

We're late! We must hurry up! *On est en retard ! Il faut qu'on se dépêche!*

▶ Pour exprimer l'**interdiction**, on peut donc utiliser *mustn't* (*must not*), *can't* (*cannot*), *may not* au présent et *couldn't* (*could not*) au passé.

We can't / mustn't take photos here. *On ne peut pas prendre de photos ici.*
Women couldn't vote then. *Les femmes n'avaient pas le droit de voter alors.*

2 La probabilité

Quand on n'est pas sûr de quelque chose, on peut utiliser *might*, *may* ou *must* selon le **degré de probabilité** de l'action.

Lina is absent: she might be sick but I saw her this morning and she seemed fine. [peu probable]
Lina is absent: we should call her, she may be sick. [probable, mais pas sûr]
Lina is very pale: she must be sick. [fort probable, presque certain]

3 Le conseil

Pour **donner des conseils**, on utilise le modal *should* (« devrais, devrait… »). À la forme négative, on emploie *shouldn't* (*should not*).

You shouldn't stay here alone. You should come with us.
Tu ne devrais pas rester seul(e) ici. Tu devrais venir avec nous.

À TON TOUR !

1 Associe chacune des phrases suivantes à la modalité qu'elle exprime.

1. I can play the guitar quite well now. •
2. Dad says I can't go out tonight. •
3. You mustn't park here. It's too dangerous. •
4. They may be already there when we arrive. •
5. I must go now, my mother's waiting for me. •
6. She could already speak English fluently at that age. •
7. Yes, you may use your camera here. •
8. He's a liar [un menteur]... but he might say the truth today. •

- • capacité
- • permission
- • obligation
- • interdiction
- • probabilité

2 Oliver est fatigué en classe et n'arrive pas à suivre les cours. Donne-lui des conseils en utilisant les expressions proposées.

sleep in class • listen to your teachers • go to bed early • play videogames late at night.

....

....

....

....

....

3 Coche le modal qui convient le mieux dans les phrases suivantes.

1. She ❑ can ❑ could ❑ may paint extremely well. She's a real artist!
2. It's very foggy tonight. You ❑ can ❑ can't ❑ must drive carefully.
3. We ❑ can ❑ may ❑ should get there on time, but I'm not sure.
4. She ❑ may ❑ might ❑ must come with us, but we shouldn't count on her.
5. ❑ Must ❑ May ❑ Could you tell me the way to the cinema please?

4 Raye le modal qui ne peut pas s'utiliser dans les phrases ci-dessous.

1. You can't / mustn't / shouldn't smoke here! It's forbidden.
2. May / Could / Must I use your phone please?
3. You don't look very well. You must / may / should see a doctor.
4. He can't /may / might be right but I don't know for sure.

CORRIGÉ p.112 D'AUTRES EXERCICES : fiche 38

L'expression de l'avenir

35

***Il existe plusieurs façons de parler de l'avenir en anglais. On peut notamment utiliser l'auxiliaire modal* will *ou* be going to.**

L'ESSENTIEL

1 *Will*

▶ *Will* est **un auxiliaire modal** (→ FICHES 33 ET 34) : il est donc invariable et suivi d'une base verbale. *Will* peut se contracter en *'ll* (après un pronom personnel en particulier) et *will not* en *won't*.

Forme affirmative	Forme négative	Forme interrogative
will + BV	*won't* + BV	*Will/Won't* + sujet + BV...?

▶ On utilise *will* quand **on se projette** dans l'avenir, quand **on est sûr** que quelque chose se produira. Il équivaut à un futur simple en français.

We'll go shopping. [projet] • She will be 14 in December. [certitude]

NB : on emploie *will* + BV dans la principale dans les phrases qui contiennent une subordonnée en *if* + présent.

If I can, I'll go with you. • We won't go out if it rains too much.

2 *Be going to*

▶ Pour exprimer le futur avec *be going to*, on conjugue l'auxiliaire *be* au présent (→ FICHE 27). Il prend la marque de la négation et se place avant le sujet dans les questions.

I'm (am) going to tell you my secret.
He isn't (is not) going to buy anything.
What are you going to do?

"I'm going to have a party for my birthday!"

▶ On utilise *be going to* pour dire que quelque chose va se produire, soit parce qu'**on en a l'intention** (on a pris une décision), soit parce qu'**un indice nous permet de le déduire**. Cela équivaut à « aller + inf. » en français.

We are going to spend our next holiday in Florida. [intention, décision]
The sky is grey, it's going to rain. [déduction liée à un indice : le ciel gris]

À RETENIR

Parler de l'avenir
→ projet, prédiction, certitude → *will* + BV
→ intention ou déduction → *be going to* + BV

À TON TOUR !

1 **Dis ce qui va se produire sur chaque image en utilisant *be going to* et les verbes proposés.**

1

2

3

4

1. .... *(leave).*
2. .... *(cross).*
3. .... *(fall).*
4. .... *(play rugby).*

2 **Fais des phrases complètes à l'aide des éléments ci-dessous.**

1. ? / be going to / you / go to London / with us

....

2. ? / you / what / will / do / tomorrow

....

3. will / not / my parents / come back / tonight

....

4. I / not / be going to / stay here

....

Pense à conjuguer *be* dans les phrases avec *be going to.*

3 **Coche la forme qui convient le mieux.**

1. If my parents agree ❑ I'm going to go ❑ I'll go to Tom's party tonight.
2. Have you decided what ❑ you're going to ❑ you'll do this summer?
3. I hope there ❑ are still going to be ❑ will still be trees in 2500.

4 **Traduis les phrases en employant *be going to* ou *will.***

1. Mon frère va se marier cet été.

....

2. Je t'appellerai demain matin.

....

3. Si nous allons à Londres, nous visiterons Hyde Park.

....

CORRIGÉ p.112

D'AUTRES EXERCICES : fiche 38

Would, could, should

36

En français, on utilise le conditionnel pour exprimer une hypothèse. En anglais, ce temps n'existe pas : on utilise des modaux (would, could, should).

L'ESSENTIEL

1 Would

▶ *Would* est le prétérit de *will*. Comme tous les modaux (→ FICHES 33 ET 34), il est **invariable**, il est suivi d'une base verbale, porte la négation et se place devant le sujet dans les questions.

Forme affirmative	Forme négative	Forme interrogative
would + BV	*wouldn't* + BV	*Would* + sujet + BV...?

NB : *would* peut se contacter en *'d*, en particulier après un pronom personnel, et *would not* en *wouldn't*.

▶ On utilise *would* + BV, comme le conditionnel français, pour envisager une **situation imaginaire ou espérée**.

It would be nice of you to come.
Ce serait sympa de ta part de venir.
If I had more money, I would buy a new car.
Si j'avais plus d'argent, j'achèterais une nouvelle voiture.

▶ On emploie *would like to* + BV pour dire ce que l'on voudrait faire ou ce que l'on aimerait que quelqu'un fasse.

What would you like to do?
Que voudrais-tu faire ?
I'd like to go to the cinema. I'd like you to come with me.
J'aimerais aller au cinéma. J'aimerais que tu viennes avec moi.

2 Could et should

▶ Il existe deux autres formes qui correspondent à des **conditionnels** français : les modaux *could* et *should* (→ FICHE 34).

« Dans *would*, *should* et *could*, on ne prononce pas le *l*. »

▶ *Could* équivaut souvent à « pourrais, pourrait… ».

Could you do that for me? *Pourrais-tu faire ca pour moi ?*
They could do that too. *Ils pourraient faire ça aussi.*

▶ *Should* se traduit quant à lui par « devrais, devrait… ».

You should work harder. *Tu devrais travailler plus dur.*
They should arrive soon. *Ils devraient arriver bientôt.*

À TON TOUR !

1 Écris des phrases complètes à l'aide des éléments proposés : utilise *if* + prétérit et *would* + BV.

1. my parents / have more free time / go on holiday

....

2. I / meet a star / take a picture

....

3. we / be richer / give money to charities

....

4. Tony / not have so much homework / go out with his friends

....

2 Observe le dessin et dis ce que voudrait Mrs Reynold pour elle et sa famille.

1. Mrs Reynold would like to ....
2. She'd like Alex to ....
3. ....
4. ....

3 Relie chaque début de phrase à la fin qui lui correspond.

1. If I were you... •
2. You don't look very well,... •
3. Do you think... •
4. I know you are hungry,... •

• a. you could help me for a few minutes?
• b. would you like a sandwich?
• c. I wouldn't leave now.
• d. you should see a doctor.

4 Traduis les phrases suivantes.

1. Qu'est-ce que je pourrais faire pour t'aider ?

....

2. Tu devrais aller chez le docteur. Tu ne devrais pas attendre.

....

3. Je serais content de les voir.

....

CORRIGÉ p.113 D'AUTRES EXERCICES : fiche 38

Base verbale ou verbe en *-ing* ?

37

L'infinitif français ne se traduit pas toujours par un infinitif en anglais. Il a trois équivalents : base verbale (BV), infinitif (to + BV) ou nom verbal (V-ing).

L'ESSENTIEL

1 La construction infinitive (BV ou *to* + BV)

▶ Avec les verbes *let* et *make*, on utilise la **base verbale seule** (BV).

My teachers make me work hard. *Mes professeurs me font travailler dur.*
Mum never lets me go out after 10 p.m.
Maman ne me laisse jamais sortir après 22 heures.

▶ Après les verbes *agree* (être d'accord), *ask*, *expect* (s'attendre à), *forget*, *need*, *refuse*, *tell* ou *want*, on utilise l'**infinitif** (*to* + BV).

My parents want to go on holiday. *Mes parents veulent partir en vacances.*
He's asking his son to tell the truth. *Il demande à son fils de dire la vérité.*
I need you to listen to me. *J'ai besoin que tu m'écoutes.*
[Tu observes que lorsque le verbe souligné est suivi d'un complément (*his son, you*), celui-ci se place avant *to* + BV]

2 Le nom verbal ou gérondif *(V-ing)*

▶ Le nom verbal permet de donner au verbe les fonctions d'un nom : il peut par exemple être **sujet d'une phrase** ou suivre **une préposition**.

Smoking is bad for your health. *Fumer est mauvais pour votre santé.*
She left without saying goodbye. *Elle est partie sans dire au revoir.*
Instead of revising, he's watching TV! *Au lieu de réviser, il regarde la télé.*

▶ On l'emploie également **après les verbes ou expressions de goût** tels que : *like*, *love*, *enjoy*, *hate*, *can't stand* / *can't bear* [ne pas supporter]…

I like dancing. • She enjoys painting. • They can't stand listening to pop music.

Avec *like*, *love*, *hate*, on peut utiliser aussi *to* + BV.

▶ On l'utilise aussi après *start*, *finish*, *stop*, *go on* / *keep* [continuer à].

You should start thinking about it. • Keep working!

ATTENTION

Avec les verbes de goût, comme like, on emploie le plus souvent V-*ing* mais on peut aussi utiliser *to* + BV. En revanche, avec *would ('d) like*, on utilise toujours *to* + BV.

I like singing (I like to sing). *J'aime chanter.*
I would like / I'd like to sing. *J'aimerais chanter.*

À TON TOUR !

1 BV ou *to* + BV ? Complète les phrases suivantes avec *to* ou note *Ø* s'il n'y a rien à ajouter.

1. My parents don't let me .... go to parties.
2. They told us .... leave immediately!
3. My sister would like .... study in the USA next year.
4. What do you expect me .... do now?
5. She makes her children .... walk the dog every day.

2 Complète les phrases en fonction de chaque illustration pour dire ce que ces gens veulent. Utilise le verbe *want*.

1. The policeman ....
2. Ben's mother ....
3. The English teacher ....
4. The children ....

turn off: *éteindre* • turn down: *baisser (le volume)* • a sweet: *un bonbon.*

3 Fais correspondre chaque début de phrase avec une fin possible.

1. She asked him...
2. She can't bear...
3. She left instead of...
4. She always makes him...
5. She said she'd like him...

- a. ... wait for her.
- b. ... to wait for her.
- c. ... waiting for him.

4 Traduis les phrases suivantes.

1. Je n'aime pas courir.

....

2. Arrête de parler! Travaille au lieu de bavarder !

....

3. Voyager est toujours une expérience intéressante.

....

CORRIGÉ p.113 D'AUTRES EXERCICES : fiche 38

Quiz express 38

Vérifie que tu as retenu les points clés des ▸ fiches 33 à 37

Réponds à chacun des quiz, puis résous l'énigme.

Le verbe (2)

1 Permission, obligation, interdiction

Fiches 33-34

Raye la phrase qui ne correspond pas au sens du panneau.

1. 

a. You must be quiet here.
b. You can be quiet here.
c. You mustn't shout [*crier*] here.

2. 

a. You can turn left.
b. You can't turn left.
c. You must turn right.

3. 

a. You are not allowed to park here.
b. You mustn't park here.
c. You are able to park here.

2 La probabilité

Fiches 33-34

Coche les phrases dans lesquelles le modal (en rose) exprime la probabilité.

☐ 1. He isn't here. He may be late.
☐ 2. I'm sad because I may never see you again.
☐ 3. May I speak to Lisa, please?
☐ 4. They said they might come too, but it was not likely.
☐ 5. I asked him if he could help me.

3 *Be going to*

Fiche 35

Explique l'emploi de *be going to* + BV dans les phrases suivantes : coche s'il s'agit d'une intention (I) ou d'une déduction (D).

1. We are going to go to Ireland in July. ☐ I ☐ D
2. He is carrying a suitcase. He is probably going to go on holiday. ☐ I ☐ D
3. Don't play ball here! You're going to break something! ☐ I ☐ D
4. I can't come with you. I'm going to visit my grandparents. ☐ I ☐ D

4 *Will ou be going to ?*

Fiche 35

Coche la forme qui convient.

1. I'm tired. I ☐ am going to ☐ will go to bed.
2. Wait for me, ☐ I'm not going to ☐ I won't be long.
3. Look at that blue sky! ☐ It's going to ☐ It'll be a beautiful day!
4. Luke ☐ is going to ☐ will call you when he gets back from school.

5 Le conditionnel

Fiche 36

Relie les éléments pour former des phrases cohérentes.

1. If I became a doctor, I... •	• a. would work harder.
2. If I become a doctor, I... •	• b. could become a doctor.
3. I think I... •	• c. will work in a hospital.
4. If you want to become a doctor, you... •	• d. would work for a humanitarian organisation.
5. If I were you, I... •	• e. should work harder.

6 *L'infinitif et le gérondif*

Fiche 37

Coche la forme du verbe qui convient.

1. Mum always makes me ☐ clear ☐ to clear ☐ clearing the table after dinner.
2. They never let us ☐ do ☐ to do ☐ doing what we want!
3. Parents want their children ☐ work ☐ to work ☐ working hard at school.
4. Please, stop ☐ complain ☐ to complain ☐ complaining all the time!
5. Don't you think ☐ dance ☐ to dance ☐ dancing is fun?
6. I need you ☐ listen ☐ to listen ☐ listening to me!

ÉNIGME

Sauras-tu déchiffrer ce célèbre proverbe anglais ?

SGGE GNIKAERB TUOHTIW ETTELEMO NA EKAM T'NAC UOY

....

You can't make an omelette without breaking eggs.

Reporte-toi aux corrigés p. 114 et calcule ton score.

Score : .../27

Les phrases négatives et interrogatives

39

Pour construire une phrase négative ou interrogative, on a besoin d'un auxiliaire. C'est lui qui porte la négation et se place avant le sujet dans les questions.

L'ESSENTIEL

1 Les phrases négatives

▶ Pour former une phrase négative, il suffit d'ajouter ***not*** à l'auxiliaire. Très souvent, on peut contracter la négation en l'accrochant à l'auxiliaire (*-n't*).

▶ L'auxiliaire est facile à trouver quand il apparaît dans les phrases affirmatives : c'est le cas de ***be, have* ou des modaux**. Quand il n'apparaît pas (présent et prétérit simples), il s'agit de ***do* ou *did***.

He is not / isn't English. • She doesn't understand anything. [présent]
You were not / weren't there. • We didn't sleep last night. [prétérit]
I have not / haven't seen you. [*present perfect*]
You must not / mustn't park here. • I will not / won't do it. [modaux]

2 Les phrases interrogatives

▶ L'**ordre** habituel des mots dans une phrase interrogative est :
(mot interrogatif) + auxiliaire + sujet + verbe + … ?

▶ Les principaux **mots interrogatifs** sont :

	interroge sur	exemples
Who	une personne	Who is your English teacher?
What	un objet, une action	What is that? What are you doing?
Where	un lieu	Where was she born?
When	un moment, une date	When did you meet her?
Whose	la possession, la parenté	Whose car is that?
How	la manière, la façon	How are you? How can you do that?

ASTUCE

Beaucoup de mots interrogatifs peuvent se construire avec *how* : *how much* interroge sur la quantité ou le prix, *how many* sur le nombre, *how old* sur l'âge, *how long* sur la durée ou la longueur, *how often* sur la fréquence et *how tall* sur la taille.

À TON TOUR !

1 Mets ces phrases à la forme négative.

1. They were very shy at the time. ....

2. I have got a sister. ....

3. They're doing the washing-up. ....

4. She eats a lot of vegetables. ....

5. My grandparents went to Mauritius last month.

....

> Quand la phrase affirmative ne comporte pas d'auxiliaire, on utilise *do* (ou *did*) à la forme négative.

2 Associe les questions et les réponses correspondantes.

1. "Are you from Ireland?" •	• **a.** "Yes, I have. I went to Glasgow in 2014."
2. "Have you ever been to Scotland?" •	• **b.** "No, I'm not. I'm from Scotland."
3. "When did you visit Scotland?" •	• **c.** "In Edinburgh, in Scotland."
4. "Where do you live?" •	• **d.** "On June 30th 2006."
5. "When were you born?" •	• **e.** "In 2014. I went to Edinburgh."

3 Lis les réponses et coche le mot interrogatif qui convient.

1. "... is your brother?" "He's 12."

❑ How ❑ How old ❑ How much ❑ How many

2. "... pupils are there in your class?" "30."

❑ How ❑ How old ❑ How much ❑ How many

3. "... does it take to go to the shopping centre?" "About 20 minutes."

❑ How much ❑ How many ❑ How long ❑ How tall

4. "... is your father?" "6 ft or 1 m 83."

❑ How old ❑ How tall ❑ How long ❑ How high

4 Trouve les questions permettant d'obtenir les réponses données.

1. "..?"

"I go to the swimming pool on Wednesdays."

2. "..?"

"Yes, I did! I visited Buckingham Palace on 6th July."

CORRIGÉ p.114 D'AUTRES EXERCICES : fiche 43

Les *question tags* et les réponses brèves

40

Les questions tags et les réponses brèves sont très courants dans les conversations en anglais. Pour les former, on a besoin d'un auxiliaire et d'un pronom personnel sujet.

L'ESSENTIEL

1 Les *questions tags*

▶ On ajoute un *question tag* à la fin d'une phrase pour **demander confirmation** de ce que l'on vient de dire (« n'est-ce pas ? », « hein ? »).

– Si la phrase est affirmative, l'auxiliaire du *tag* est négatif et contracté.

You're (are) very tall for your age, aren't you?
(+) (−)
Jane can play the harp, can't she?

– Si la phrase est négative, l'auxiliaire du *tag* est affirmatif (non contracté).

You aren't very patient, are you?
(−) (+)
They have never been to New York, have they?
Chris doesn't love her anymore, does he?

▶ On peut aussi utiliser un *tag* en réaction à ce qui vient d'être dit, pour **exprimer son étonnement** (« Ah bon ? », « Vraiment ? »). Dans ce cas, le *tag* est à la même forme que la phrase à laquelle on réagit.

"I like green beans." "Do you?" [phrase affirmative → tag affirmatif]
"I don't like fruit." "Don't you?" [phrase négative → tag négatif]

ATTENTION

Dans les phrases affirmatives au présent et prétérit simples, l'auxiliaire n'apparaît pas. Pour former les *tags*, il faut donc penser à utiliser *do(n't)* ou *does(n't)* au présent simple et *did(n't)* au prétérit simple.

2 Les réponses brèves

On ne se contente pas de répondre *Yes* ou *No* à une *yes/no question* : on complète sa réponse **en reprenant l'auxiliaire de la question**.

"Are his parents American?" "Yes, they are. / No, they aren't."
"Do you like Maths?" "Yes, I do. / No, I don't."
"Has Ben got a bike?" "Yes, he has. / No, he hasn't."

À TON TOUR !

1 **Réagis avec surprise à ce que te dit Theo. Coche le *tag* qui convient.**

1. "My mother is a doctor."

❑ "Is she?" ❑ "Isn't she?" ❑ "Has she?" ❑ "Does she?"

2. "I've got a younger sister."

❑ "Has she?" ❑ "Hasn't she?" ❑ "Have you?" ❑ "Haven't you?"

3. "I can play the drums and the piano."

❑ "Can I?" ❑ "Can they?" ❑ "Can you?" ❑ "Can't you?"

4. "We went to Hawaii last summer."

❑ "Do we?" ❑ "Do you?" ❑ "Didn't you?" ❑ "Did you?"

2 **Observe le *question tag* puis complète la première partie de la phrase par l'auxiliaire manquant.**

1. Tom .... always very nice with her, isn't he?
2. Alex .... play the guitar very well, can't he?
3. He .... played for long, has he?
4. The children .... be more careful, shouldn't they?
5. Emma .... work on Wednesdays, does she?

3 **Demande confirmation en ajoutant un *question tag*.**

1. You're interested in languages, ...?
2. Your parents can't speak English, ...?
3. Your sister doesn't live with your family, ...?
4. She lives in the USA, ...?
5. Your brother visited her last summer, ...?

4 **Tu interroges Tony. Associe tes questions aux réponses brèves qu'il te donne. Il restera une réponse brève : à toi d'imaginer une question.**

1. Have you got a few minutes to answer me? •	• a. Yes, I am.
2. Are you a student here? •	• b. No, she doesn't.
3. Does your boyfriend go to the same school as you? •	• c. Yes, I have.
4. Do your friends often spend time with you? •	• d. No, they don't.
5. Would the students here like to have more free time? •	• e. Yes, they did.
6. .... •	• f. Yes, they would.

CORRIGÉ p.115 D'AUTRES EXERCICES : fiche 43

Les phrases exclamatives

41

Une phrase exclamative permet d'exprimer une émotion : surprise, incrédulité, admiration... La structure de la phrase dépend de la nature des mots sur lesquels porte l'exclamation.

L'ESSENTIEL

1 Avec un adjectif ou un adverbe

▶ On peut former une exclamative avec ***how*** **+ adjectif ou adverbe**. On peut éventuellement terminer la phrase par un sujet et un verbe conjugué.

How funny (this is)! *Comme / Que c'est drôle !*
How fast he drives! *Comme / Qu'est-ce qu'il conduit vite !*

▶ Après un groupe verbal, on peut utiliser ***so*** **+ adjectif ou adverbe**.

This is so funny! *C'est si/tellement drôle !*
He's driving so fast! *Il conduit si/tellement vite !*

2 Avec un nom ou un groupe nominal

▶ Si l'exclamation porte sur un nom ou un groupe nominal, on peut utiliser ***what*** **+ GN**. Si le nom est un dénombrable singulier, il est précédé de l'article *a(n)* ; sinon, il n'y a pas d'article.

What a mess! *Quel désordre !*
What a beautiful house (you have)!
Quelle belle maison (vous avez) !
What luck (they have)! *Quelle chance (ils ont) !*

▶ Après un groupe verbal, on peut employer ***such*** **+ GN**.

You have such a beautiful house!
Vous avez une si belle maison !
They have such luck!
Ils ont une telle chance !

ASTUCE

Pour ne pas confondre les exclamatives en *how* et *what* avec des phrases interrogatives (→ FICHE 39), prête attention à l'**ordre des mots** : dans une question, le sujet et le verbe sont inversés.

What a strange story (he told)! *Quelle histoire étrange (il a racontée) !*
What story did he tell? *Quelle histoire a-t-il racontée ?*
How old he is! *Comme il est vieux !*
How old is he? *Quel âge a-t-il ?*

À TON TOUR !

1 Complète les phrases suivantes avec *so* ou *such*.

1. The history courses I take are .... interesting! My history teacher is .... a fascinating man!
2. I've had .... a good time in London! I've never had .... fun! I'm .... happy!
3. My neighbours are .... strange people! I feel .... uncomfortable when I meet them!

2 Associe les éléments pour former cinq exclamatives différentes.

What •	• a •	• pretty she is!
How •	• an •	• complicated story!
	• Ø •	• enormous cake you've made!
		• quickly you did your homework!
		• eccentric clothes she's wearing today!

3 Sur le London Eye, Amy est très impressionnée. Écris ses exclamations avec les mots proposés (en variant les tournures !).

awesome • nice view • beautiful city • high • impressive buildings

1. ....
2. ....
3. ....
4. ....
5. ....

Observe bien la nature des mots (GN, adjectif ou adverbe) et le nombre (singulier ou pluriel) des noms avant de choisir les exclamations qui conviennent.

4 Ajoute la ponctuation finale (! ou ?) en fonction du type de phrase, exclamative ou interrogative.

1. How tall your father is...
2. How tall are you...
3. What present will you bring her for her birthday...
4. What nice presents she got for her birthday...
5. How expensive these jeans are...

CORRIGÉ p.115 D'AUTRES EXERCICES : fiche 43

Les subordonnées relatives

Une proposition relative commence par un pronom relatif et complète un nom que l'on appelle son antécédent. Les pronoms relatifs les plus courants sont **who, which, that** *et* **whose.**

L'ESSENTIEL

1 Les relatives introduites par *who, which, that*

▶ Le choix du pronom dépend de **l'antécédent** : si c'est une personne, on utilise *who* (ou *that* à l'oral) ; sinon, on emploie *which* ou *that*.

The boy who/that is watching us is my son. *Le garçon qui nous regarde...*
I love the painting which/that is there. *... le tableau qui est ici.*

▶ Si le pronom est **sujet** du verbe de la relative (« qui » en français), il est obligatoire. En revanche, s'il est **complément** du verbe de la relative (« que »), on l'utilise rarement.

The man who saw us yesterday... *L'homme qui nous a vus hier...*
[*who* est le sujet de *saw* : il est donc nécessaire.]

The man Ø we saw yesterday... *L'homme que nous avons vu hier...*
[Le sujet de *saw* est *we* : le pronom relatif peut être omis.]

▶ Quand le verbe de la relative est **suivi d'une préposition**, celle-ci reste à côté du verbe et on omet le plus souvent le pronom relatif.

I was talking to a woman. → The woman Ø I was talking to...
You are looking for a book. → The book Ø you are looking for...

2 Les relatives introduites par *whose*

▶ Le pronom relatif *whose* peut s'utiliser quel que soit l'antécédent. Il est **complément du nom** et exprime le plus souvent la possession ou un lien de parenté. On le traduit par « dont ».

▶ Il est immédiatement suivi d'un GN.

Emma is the girl whose parents won the lottery yesterday.
The company whose head office is in my city is specialized in computers.

ASTUCE

Whose s'utilise comme le génitif (→ FICHE 24) ; il est donc entre deux noms et ne peut être suivi d'un déterminant.

Tom's father is a doctor. *Le père de Tom est docteur.*
Tom, whose father is a doctor, lives near the hospital.
Tom, dont le père est docteur, vit près de l'hôpital.

À TON TOUR !

1 **Dans les phrases ci-dessous, le relatif *that* a été systématiquement employé. Coche le pronom par lequel il pourrait être remplacé.**

1. We haven't seen the new pupil <u>that</u> comes from London. ❑ who ❑ which
2. I really liked the chocolate cake <u>that</u> you made yesterday. ❑ who ❑ which
3. He has broken the chair <u>that</u> is in the office. ❑ who ❑ which
4. Julia is my English friend <u>that</u> now lives in France. ❑ who ❑ which

2 **Raye, si nécessaire, les pronoms relatifs qui ne peuvent pas s'utiliser dans les phrases suivantes.**

1. Do you know the people who / that / which live next to your grandparents'?
2. The film who / that / Ø we've just watched is very funny!
3. I don't know the man who / that / Ø works with my father.
4. I don't know the man who /that / Ø we've just met in front of your house.
5. The book who / which / Ø she gave me for my birthday is really boring.
6. I have read all the books which / that / Ø are on my shelves.

3 **Remets ces mots dans l'ordre pour écrire une phrase complète contenant une proposition relative. Puis souligne celle-ci.**

1. are / The children / I / looked / last weekend / very / polite. / after

....

2. we / about / The exam / difficult. / are / is / really / talking

....

3. in / is / my grandmother / The school / studied / building. / very old / a

....

Chaque verbe est immédiatement suivi d'une préposition.

4 **À partir des deux phrases proposées, écris-en une seule contenant une proposition relative introduite par *whose*.**

1. Ray has come to drive us back home. His car is parked in front of the school.

....

2. I have never met this man. The man's wife is a famous actress.

....

3. Cathy lives just next door. I don't know her family yet.

....

Cherche un génitif ou un possessif pour savoir où introduire *whose*.

CORRIGÉ p.116 D'AUTRES EXERCICES : fiche 43

Quiz express

Vérifie que tu as retenu les points clés des fiches 39 à 42

43

Réponds à chacun des quiz, puis résous l'énigme.

La phrase

1 Les phrases interrogatives

Fiche 38

Coche le mot interrogatif qui manque dans la question.

1. "... did you go last weekend?" "I went to Brighton."
   - ☐ Who ☐ Where ☐ When ☐ How long
2. "... people were there at the concert?" "Probably more than a thousand."
   - ☐ How old ☐ How long ☐ How much ☐ How many
3. "... school bag is that?" "I think it's Abby's."
   - ☐ Whose ☐ Who ☐ What ☐ How much
4. "... does he do judo?" "Three times a week."
   - ☐ When ☐ Where ☐ How often ☐ How many

2 Les phrases négatives

Fiche 38

Associe chaque phrase affirmative à son contraire, c'est-à-dire à la phrase négative correspondante.

1. He'd like to eat Indian food. •
2. He can eat Indian food. •
3. He likes Indian food. •
4. He ate Indian food. •

- • a. He doesn't like Indian food.
- • b. He wouldn't like to eat Indian food.
- • c. He can't eat Indian food.
- • d. He won't eat Indian food.
- • e. He didn't eat Indian food.

3 Les *question tags*

Fiche 39

Coche le *question tag* qui convient.

1. You don't really like French, ☐ don't you? ☐ do you? ☐ are you?
2. Tom goes to school at 8 am, ☐ doesn't he? ☐ does he? ☐ isn't he?
3. His parents lived abroad for two years, ☐ didn't he? ☐ have they? ☐ didn't they?
4. Olivia will come with us, ☐ won't she? ☐ wouldn't she? ☐ isn't she?
5. They haven't seen her for weeks, ☐ haven't they? ☐ have they? ☐ did they?

4 Les réponses brèves

Fiche 39

Coche, pour chaque question, la réponse brève qui ne convient pas.

1. "Have they got a new car?"

☐ a. "Yes, they have." ☐ b. "No, they haven't." ☐ c. "Yes, they are."

2. "Are you French?"

☐ a. "Yes, you are." ☐ b. "Yes, I am." ☐ c. "No, I'm not."

3. "Did he do the exercise?"

☐ a. "Yes, he did." ☐ b. "Yes, he has." ☐ c. "No, he didn't."

4. "Does your mother speak English?"

☐ a. "Yes, she can." ☐ b. "Yes, she does." ☐ c. "No, she doesn't."

5 Les subordonnées relatives

Fiche 41

Entoure le relatif qui convient parmi les deux propositions.

1. Do you know the boy who / which takes the bus with us every Monday?
2. Do you know the man who / whose wife is a Scottish writer?
3. The book Ø / who I have just read is fantastic!
4. The phone who / which has been left on the desk is probably the teacher's.
5. He's the guy Ø / whose she fell in love with.
6. All Ø / that glitters is not gold. [« Tout ce qui brille n'est pas or. »]

ÉNIGME

Trouve le nom de ce grand écrivain irlandais à l'aide des indices.

- My first name is also a golden statuette that movie stars receive as an Academy award.
- My surname sounds like an adjective describ-ing an animal that is not domesticated.
- My most famous novel is *The Picture of Dorian Gray* (1890).

Who am I?

Oscar Wilde

Reporte-toi aux corrigés p. 116 et calcule ton score.

Score : .../23

Langages

L'influence du français dans la langue anglaise

44

On pense souvent que notre langue emprunte beaucoup à l'anglais mais le français a lui aussi marqué la culture et la langue outre-Manche. Environ 30% des mots anglais viendraient du français.

The role of the Normans

The Bayeux tapestry tells the story of the conquest of England by **William the Conqueror**, Duke of Normandy, and **the Normans**.

After **the battle of Hastings (1066)**, William became the King of England and gave important positions and estates to Normans, who spoke French. That's why there are many French words in English, especially in the fields of government, justice and law, food, fashion and culture.

La tapisserie de Bayeux raconte l'histoire de la conquête de l'Angleterre par Guillaume le Conquérant, duc de Normandie, et les Normands.

Après la bataille de Hastings (1066), Guillaume devint roi d'Angleterre et donna des positions et des propriétés importantes à des Normands, qui parlaient français. C'est pourquoi il y a beaucoup de mots français en anglais, en particulier dans les domaines du gouvernement, de la justice et de la loi, de la nourriture, de la mode et de la culture.

Meat

At the time of the Normans, **the people from the English upper class** who spoke French, were also those who ate meat. On the contrary, **the ordinary people**, who raised the animals, spoke in their Saxon language. That's why there are two different words in English to talk about the meat and the animal.

Animals	Meat
cow [vache], ox [bœuf]	beef
calf [veau]	veal
pig [cochon, porc]	pork
sheep [mouton]	mutton

À l'époque des Normands, les gens de la haute société anglaise, qui parlaient français, étaient aussi ceux qui mangeaient de la viande. Au contraire, les gens ordinaires qui élevaient les animaux parlaient leur langue saxonne. C'est pourquoi il y a deux mots différents en anglais pour parler de la viande et de l'animal.

Sports

Many sports names come from England… but not all of them! **The word sport** itself comes from an Old French word meaning "amusement" (desport).

In the Middle Ages, there was a popular game in France called **"jeu de paume"** (game of the palm): the players threw a ball back and forth, striking it with the palm of the hand. The server said "tenez !" to let his opponent know he was ready to play, and… that's where the word "tennis" comes from!

Beaucoup de noms de sports viennent d'Angleterre… mais pas tous ! Le mot sport lui-même vient d'un mot en ancien français signifiant « amusement » (*desport*).
Au Moyen Âge, il y avait un jeu populaire en France, le jeu de paume : les joueurs s'échangeaient une balle en la frappant avec la paume de la main. Le serveur disait « Tenez ! » pour signaler à son adversaire qu'il était prêt à jouer, et… c'est de là que vient le mot « tennis » !

QUIZ

Les affirmations suivantes sont-elles vraies (true) ou fausses (false) ? Coche la case appropriée.

	True	False
1. The Normans conquered England in the 11th century.	❑	❑
2. The Normans spoke English very well.	❑	❑
3. The word beef was invented by Saxon farmers.	❑	❑
4. The word tennis comes from a French word.	❑	❑

1. True ; 2. False ; 3. False ; 4. True

École et société
À la découverte de sports typiquement britanniques

45

Beaucoup de sports nés en Grande-Bretagne (football, rugby, golf...) sont devenus populaires dans le monde entier. Mais certains sports moins connus sont pourtant très appréciés des Britanniques.

Cricket

Cricket is England's national sport. In the spring and summer, it is played in most villages and towns on Sundays. The teams are made up of eleven players each who play with **a ball and a bat.** The official rules were established in 1835 but British people often say they are too complicated to be understood by foreigners! Yet, cricket is also **very popular in many** former **British colonies**.

Le cricket est le sport national de l'Angleterre. Au printemps et en été, on y joue dans la plupart des villages et des villes le dimanche. Les équipes sont constituées de 11 joueurs chacune qui jouent avec une balle et une batte. Les règles officielles ont été établies en 1835 mais les Britanniques disent souvent qu'elles sont trop compliquées pour être comprises par des étrangers ! Pourtant, le cricket est aussi très populaire dans beaucoup d'anciennes colonies britanniques.

Bowls (or lawn bowls)

Lawn bowls consists in **rolling your bowls close to the white ball** (called Jack) and is played on a green. It is one of Britain's oldest sports. It was so popular in England in the Middle Ages that it was seen as a threat to archery. Since archery was essential to the national defense, playing bowls was **forbidden by law** in 1361. However, the ban didn't concern Scotland where the game developed and is still **very popular**.

Le boulingrin (jeu de boules sur gazon) consiste à faire rouler ses boules près de la boule blanche (nommée Jack) et se joue sur gazon. C'est un des plus vieux sports britanniques. Il était si populaire en Angleterre au Moyen Âge qu'il fut considéré comme une menace pour le tir à l'arc. Comme le tir à l'arc était essentiel pour la défense nationale, le boulingrin fut interdit par la loi en 1361. Cependant, l'interdiction ne concernait pas l'Écosse où le jeu s'est développé et reste encore très populaire.

Rowing

Rowing is **a very old British sport**. The first modern races in England date back from the 10th century. **The Boat Race**, a famous rowing race between two crews from Oxford and Cambridge (Britain's oldest and most prestigious universities), is considered one of the biggest sporting events in London. It started in 1829 and has been held every year since 1857 **on the river Thames** with more than 250,000 people watching from the banks and millions on television.

L'aviron est un sport britannique très ancien. Les premières courses modernes en Angleterre datent du xe siècle. *The Boat Race*, une célèbre course d'aviron entre deux équipes d'Oxford et de Cambridge (les universités les plus anciennes et les plus prestigieuses de Grande-Bretagne), est considérée comme un des plus grands événements sportifs à Londres. Elle débuta en 1829 et a lieu chaque année depuis 1857 sur la Tamise, avec près de 250 000 spectateurs sur les berges du fleuve et plusieurs millions à la télévision.

QUIZ

Relie chaque phrase au(x) sport(s) qu'elle concerne.

1. It was forbidden in England. •
2. It is played on a green. •
3. A famous race is held on the Thames every year. •
4. It is the national sport of England. •
5. It is more popular in Scotland than in the rest of Britain. •
6. Each team has eleven players. •

• a. cricket
• b. bowls
• c. rowing

1.b ; 2.a et b ; 3.c ; 4.a ; 5.b ; 6.a.

Voyages et migrations
La ville de New York

46

Située sur la côte Est des États-Unis, New York est la ville la plus grande et la plus peuplée du pays. C'est aussi la plus visitée !

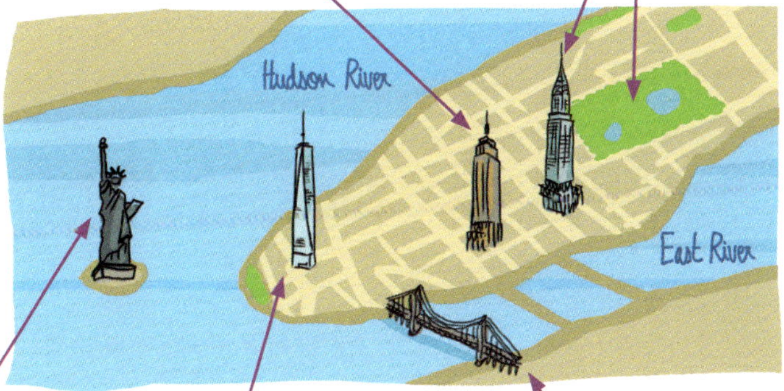

New York City is made up of **five districts or boroughs**: Manhattan, Brooklyn, the Bronx, Queens and Staten Island. But its most diverse and famous district is definitely **the island of Manhattan**, where the history of the city started.

Indeed, the island has been inhabited for very long. The Lenape Indians were its first inhabitants and gave it its name "Manhattan". In 1626, the Dutch bought the island for the equivalent of $24 and called it New Amsterdam. In 1664, the British conquered the place and gave it a new name: New York.

New York City est composée de cinq quartiers ou arrondissements : Manhattan, Brooklyn, le Bronx, le Queens, et Staten Island. Mais son quartier le plus varié et le plus célèbre est sans aucun doute l'île de Manhattan où l'histoire de la ville a commencé.

En effet, l'île est habitée depuis très longtemps. Les Indiens Lenapes furent ses premiers habitants et lui donnèrent son nom « Manhattan ». En 1626, les Hollandais achetèrent l'île pour l'équivalent de 24 dollars et l'appelèrent New Amsterdam. En 1664, les Britanniques conquirent l'endroit et lui donnèrent un nouveau nom : New York.

Iconic monuments and places

The Statue of Liberty

"Liberty Enlightening the World" was a **present from** the people of **France** to the United States for the centenary of the American independence. It was made by sculptor F. Bartholdi and engineer Gustave Eiffel and was inaugurated in 1886. It has become a symbol of the USA and of freedom throughout the world.

« La Liberté éclairant le monde » est un cadeau du peuple français aux États-Unis pour le centenaire de l'indépendance américaine. Elle a été édifiée par le sculpteur Frédéric Bartholdi et l'ingénieur Gustave Eiffel et inaugurée en 1886. Elle est devenue un symbole des États-Unis et de la liberté à travers le monde.

The Empire State Building

The Empire State Building (ESB) is New York City's **most famous skyscraper**. When it was built, in 1931, it was the highest building in the world. It is 381 metres high and has 102 stories. Millions of people visit it for its spectacular view.

L'Empire State Building (ESB) est le plus célèbre gratte-ciel de New York. Quand il fut construit, en 1931, il était le plus haut bâtiment du monde. Il fait 381 mètres de haut et a 102 étages. Des millions de gens le visitent pour sa vue spectaculaire.

Central Park

Located in the heart of Manhattan, Central Park was America's first landscaped **public park**. It opened in 1858 and was expanded until 1873. Its area is now 341 ha! There are hundreds of attractions: baseball fields, an ice-skating rink, horse-drawn carriages… and even a zoo!

Situé au cœur de Manhattan, Central Park fut le premier parc paysager public en Amérique. Il ouvrit en novembre 1858 et fut agrandi jusqu'en 1873. Sa surface est maintenant de 341 ha ! Il y a des centaines d'attractions : des terrains de baseball, une patinoire, des calèches… et même un zoo !

QUIZ

Coche la ou les bonne(s) réponse(s).

1. The most famous district of New York is…

❑ a. Brooklyn ❑ b. the Bronx ❑ c. Queens ❑ d. Manhattan

2. The statue of Liberty was offered to the USA by…

❑ a. the Indians ❑ b. France ❑ c. American independantists

3. In Central Park, you can…

❑ a. leave Manhattan ❑ b. play sport ❑ c. visit a zoo ❑ d. relax

1. d ; 2. b ; 3. b, c, d

Rencontre avec une autre culture
Jours fériés et fêtes traditionnelles en Amérique

47

On connaît Halloween, mais d'autres fêtes américaines sont bien plus populaires encore. Elles sont liées à l'histoire et aux fondements de l'Amérique.

Thanksgiving

In the USA, Thanksgiving Day is the **fourth Thursday in November**. On that day most American families get together and share a nice dinner with roast turkey, cranberry sauce, potatoes and pumpkin pie.

The first Thanksgiving was celebrated in Plymouth (New England) in 1621. **The Pilgrim fathers** had arrived from England in December 1620, on a ship called the *Mayflower*. The winter was really harsh and many of them died. But the Indians helped them and in the fall 1621, after a very successful harvest, the Pilgrims decided to have **a feast to thank God and the Indians**.

Aux États-Unis, Thanksgiving est le 4e jeudi de novembre. Ce jour-là, la plupart des familles américaines se retrouvent et partagent un bon dîner avec de la dinde rôtie, de la sauce aux canneberges, des pommes de terre et de la tarte à la citrouille.
Le premier Thanksgiving fut célébré à Plymouth (Nouvelle Angleterre) en 1621. Les pères pèlerins étaient arrivés d'Angleterre en décembre 1620, sur un bateau appelé le *Mayflower*. L'hiver fut très rigoureux et beaucoup d'entre eux moururent. Mais les Indiens les aidèrent et à l'automne 1621, après une très bonne récolte, les pèlerins décidèrent de faire un festin pour remercier Dieu et les Indiens.

Independence Day (July 4th)

Independence Day is the anniversary of the publication of **the Declaration of Independence from Great Britain in 1776**, that is to say the day when the USA was born as an independent nation.

On July 4th, many people have picnics or barbecues with their family and friends and display **the American flag** outside their homes. There are also public ceremonies, baseball games, parades, concerts and shows… and more than 14,000 **firework displays** across the country!

Le jour de l'indépendance est l'anniversaire de la publication de la déclaration d'Indépendance par rapport à la Grande-Bretagne en 1776, c'est-à-dire le jour où les États-Unis sont nés en tant que nation indépendante.
Le 4 juillet, beaucoup de gens font des pique-niques ou des barbecues avec leur famille et leurs amis et déploient le drapeau américain à l'extérieur de leur maison. Il y a aussi des cérémonies publiques, des matchs de baseball, des défilés, des concerts et des spectacles... et plus de 14 000 feux d'artifice à travers le pays !

Martin Luther King Day

Martin Luther King Day is on **the third Monday of January**. It celebrates the life and achievements of Martin Luther King (MLK), a famous Black American **civil rights leader** who fought for racial equality in the United States in the 1960s. Like Gandhi who inspired him, he believed in **non-violent protest** and received the Nobel Peace Prize in 1964. He was assassinated four years later. MLK Day has been a national holiday since 1983. It is still important in today's America **to promote equal rights** for all Americans.

Le jour de Martin Luther King est le 3e lundi de janvier. Il commémore la vie et les réalisations de Martin Luther King, célèbre dirigeant noir américain du mouvement des droits civiques qui combattit pour l'égalité raciale aux États-Unis dans les années 1960. Comme Gandhi qui l'inspira, il croyait à la contestation non violente et reçut le prix Nobel de la paix en 1964. Il fut assassiné quatre ans plus tard.
Le jour de MLK est un jour férié depuis 1983. Il est toujours important dans l'Amérique d'aujourd'hui pour promouvoir l'égalité des droits pour tous les Américains.

QUIZ

Coche les affirmations vraies.

- ❑ **1.** Thanksgiving is celebrated in November.
- ❑ **2.** The first Thanksgiving meal took place in 1776.
- ❑ **3.** The USA became an independent country in 1776.
- ❑ **4.** There are many public events in the USA on July 4th.
- ❑ **5.** Martin Luther King Day has been a holiday since he was killed in 1968.

1, 3 et 4 sont vraies.

CORRIGÉS des quiz et des exercices

Fiche 1

1re écoute

1. c • 2. a • 3. c • 4. b.

2e écoute

1. "Go all the way down this street. At the corner turn right. At the supermarket, 'Jenny's shop', cross the street and turn left."
2. "Continue straight on and just before the roundabout, take Lauren Street on your left.

Fiche 2

1re écoute

1. b • 2. b • 3. a • 4. c.

2e écoute

1. "*Titanic* is one of my favourite films and I can watch it again and again."
2. "I'm crazy about DiCaprio as Jack, and I adore Winslet as Rose."
3. "I always cry when the ship breaks apart."
4. "The final scene is very impressive too."

Fiche 3

1re écoute

1. c • 2. a • 3. a • 4. b.

2e écoute

1. b • 2. b • 3. a • 4 b.

Fiche 4

1re écoute

1. a • 2. b • 3. c.

2e écoute

1. Emma agrees; "I agree with you on that point."
2. Ian agrees: "I must admit."
3. Emma agrees: "You're right."
4. Emma disagrees: "Oh, come on!"

Fiche 5

Quiz express

1. July 4th in Chicago

1. a • 2. b • 3. b • 4. a • 5. b • 6. c • 7. b • 8. c.

Le script

My name is Renata. I'm from the United States. I live in Chicago. July 4th is Independence Day in the United States. I love July 4th because there's always a celebration. The weather is really warm. I usually go down to Navy Pier where the water is. There's always a parade by Navy Pier with fireworks. People celebrate by bringing food and drinks. We party, we dance, and we celebrate the birth of our Nation. July 4th is a really nice time for people to barbecue. There are usually parties going on. I like to visit my family and friends and party with them. It's a great time to visit Chicago because we usually have the "Taste of Chicago" where all different restaurants come and bring their food for people to taste. You should come to Chicago on the 4th of July.

[Je m'appelle Renata. Je viens des États-Unis. J'habite à Chicago. Le 4 juillet est le jour de l'indépendance aux États-Unis. J'adore le 4 juillet parce qu'il y a toujours une fête. Il fait chaud. Je vais généralement à Navy Pier, au bord de l'eau. Il y a toujours un défilé le long de Navy Pier, avec des feux d'artifice. Les gens apportent à manger et à boire. On fait la fête, on danse et on célèbre la naissance de notre nation. Le 4 juillet est une bonne occasion de faire un barbecue. Des fêtes sont organisées. J'aime bien rendre visite à ma famille et à mes amis et faire la fête avec eux. C'est un bon moment pour visiter Chicago car il y a le *Taste of Chicago*, (un festival) auquel tous les restaurants participent et apportent leur nourriture pour la faire goûter aux gens. Tu devrais venir à Chicago pour le 4 juillet !]

2. English breakfast

1. b • **2.** c • **3.** c • **4.** c • **5.** b • **6.** c.

Le script

Hmmm so... The English breakfast is very popular in England. Although people think we eat that every morning, this is not true. It's mostly for special occasions or if you have guests around. A lot of people eat it as brunch, so breakfast and lunch, maybe on a Sunday. And then you have a roast later on in the day. It consists of lots of different things. You can choose what you want, but the "available" foods are black pudding, mushrooms, tomatoes, toast, eggs, bacon, baked beans and hash browns.

[Le petit-déjeuner anglais est très populaire en Angleterre. Les gens croient qu'on mange cela tous les matins, mais ce n'est pas vrai. C'est surtout pour les grandes occasions ou s'il y a des invités. Beaucoup de gens le mangent en guise de brunch, donc à la fois petit-déjeuner et déjeuner, par exemple le dimanche. Et ensuite on mange un rôti plus tard dans la journée. Le petit-déjeuner anglais se compose de différents éléments. On peut choisir ce que l'on veut mais les aliments proposés sont souvent : du boudin noir, des champignons, des tomates, du pain grillé, des œufs, du bacon, des haricots à la sauce tomate et des pommes de terre rissolées.]

Fiche 6 Expression orale

"Hey Mona, did you enjoy the concert last night?"

"Oh, yes, it was awesome!"

"I really appreciate the Big Boys' band."

"Me too. They must rehearse a lot to be so good!"

"I agree with you. I guess they have fantastic studios where they can work on their songs."

"Did you see how many people clapped their hands when the band came on stage?"

"I was really impressed! But I will understand why girls scream so much."

"Well I guess it's because they are all in love with the singers."

Fiche 7 Expression orale

I'm really excited because, next month, I'm going to go to the mountains with my Dad. We love skiing, so, I think we will do that all day long.
We are also planning to visit some friends who live in the Alps: it's going to be lots of fun to meet with them again.
It will be fantastic just to relax and to forget all about school and homework!
I would love to ask you to come along with us, but my father says not this year. He promised it would be for next year.

Fiche 8 Expression orale

"Hello Miss! Can I help you?"

"Yes, please. I'm looking for a t-shirt."

"What size are you?"

"I'm size Large."

"OK. Do you like this one?"

"Yes, I like it. Can I try it on?"

"Of course, the fitting-room is on your right."

"Awesome! It fits me perfectly! I'll take it."

Fiche 9 Expression orale

1. f • **2.** d • **3.** a • **4.** g • **5.** b • **6.** c • **7.** e.

Fiche 10 Quiz express

Voici des propositions de réponses :

1. How sporty are you?

I love sport! I think sport is interesting and necessary. I practise sport at school and on Saturdays. When I practise sport, I feel good. I prefer to go jogging all alone so I can do what I want. When my father asks me to go for a bicycle ride, I accept with joy. I usually work out with my friends because it's more fun.

2. What do you like about your friends?

I have many friends and I like them because they are nice. It's always fun to be with them. My friends must listen to me and understand me. When I'm with my friends, I feel great. Their friendship is precious because we can laugh together. I love to go out with them. I see them every weekend and we talk for hours! I also want my friends to be happy around me, and to tell me their secrets. And of course, I don't want them to be aggressive with me or to make fun of me.

Fiche 11 Compréhension écrite

1. **1.** b. their national day: *leur fête nationale*
   2. c. bad-tempered: *qui a mauvais caractère*
   3. b. a shoemaker: *un cordonnier*

4. c. barter: *troquer*

5. b. treasure: *trésor*

6. a. vanish: *disparaître*.

2. 1. False [they aren't people, they are fairies] ; 2. False • 3. True • 4. True • 5. True.

Fiche 12 Compréhension écrite

1. Le bon ordre est : f – d – b – e – a – c.

2. 1. False • 2. True • 3. True • 4. True • 5. False.

Fiche 13 Compréhension écrite

1. 1. a. before • b. before • c. after.

   2. a. before • b. after • c. after.

2. Il fallait cocher les phrases : 1, 2, 4 et 6.

Fiche 14 Compréhension écrite

1. Il fallait cocher les phrases : 1, 3, 5, 6 et 9.

2. According to Chloe, the main arguments are 5 and 6 [arguments précédés de *most*]

Fiche 15 Quiz express

1. Comprendre les mots inconnus

1. adj., a • 2. verbe, c • 3. nom, a • 4. nom, b.

2. Comprendre les informations essentielles

1. c et d • 2. a, b et e • 3. b et c • 4. b.

3. Comprendre les détails

1. False [she's worried about her son] • 2. True • 3. True • 4. False [this is the first time] • 5. True • 6. False [he's putting out a message for his colleagues to look for him] • 7. True.

Fiche 16 Expression écrite

This photograph was taken by Bjørn Hovdal, a Norwegian photographer. It is simply entitled "London bus and cab" but it shows more than a bus and a taxi: it is a typical view of Westminster and Big Ben.

The picture is in black and white except for the red double-decker bus. In the foreground, we can see a black cab in the middle and two police officers on horses on the right. In the background, there are the Houses of Parliament and London's famous clock tower: Big Ben.

Fiche 17 Expression écrite

I remember the Christmas I spent in Australia when I was 10.

At the time, my uncle used to live in Sydney; so it was a great opportunity to spend

Christmas in the sun. We took the plane from Paris on December 23rd and arrived in Sydney 24 hours later, on December 24th. After a good night's sleep, when I woke up on Christmas Day, the sun was shining and there were presents everywhere in the garden! After opening our présents, my cousins and I played with our new toys for hours. While we were playing, my parents and uncle were preparing everything to have a BBQ party on the beach.
I had a wonderful time, and I'll never forget the only Xmas I spent in my swimming shorts!

Fiche 18 Expression écrite

1. I don't make friends easily, so I have got only one close friend. Her name is Lisa and she lives in Paris, just like me. We go to the same school and we have the same tastes: we both like playing tennis and reading fantasy books but we don't like listening to rap music.

   I know Lisa isn't always perfect: she can be a bit lazy and jealous sometimes, but I don't care because she is the nicest person I know and the best friend in the world!

2. 1. hardworking
   2. clever, intelligent
   3. mean, nasty
   4. generous

Fiche 19 Expression écrite

In the past, when my grandparents were young for example, people didn't have any computers and still, most children were happy. So we can ask ourselves / wonder why children can't even imagine living without a smartphone or a tablet nowadays.

I'm a teenager myself, but I agree I with the people who say that young people spend too much time on screens.

My brother is the best (or worst!) example I have. Indeed, he spends his time playing on his tablet all day.

To tell the truth, I worry about him and children in general: in my opinion/to my mind new technology can change them into antisocial beings or even zombies. That's why I think parents should be very careful.

Fiche 20 Expression écrite

Hi Alex,

Thanks for inviting me! I don't really like hiking, but I would love to go moutain biking. Canoeing sounds great too.

See you soon,

Ethan

Fiche 21 Quiz express

1. Décrire une image

in the middle: 1 • in the top right-hand corner: 6 • at the top: 2 • at the bottom: 3 • on the right: 4 • on the left: 5.

2. Raconter un souvenir d'enfance

L'ordre correct est : e – b – d – g – c – a – h – f.

3. Rédiger le portrait de quelqu'un

1. My brother Alex is 3 years older than me.
2. He loves playing the guitar.
3. He doesn't like the same things as me.
4. But we like playing tennis together.
5. I think he is the laziest person in the family.
6. But he is also the nicest brother in the world.

4. Argumenter sur un thème

1. we can ask why • **2.** to think • **3.** in my opinion • **4.** in addition • **5.** in fact • **6.** for example

5. Écrire un courriel

Il fallait rayer: **1.** a. et b. • **2.** c. et d. • **3.** a. et b. • **4.** a. et b.

Fiche 22 À ton tour !

1. **1.** I've got two pets a cat and a hamster.
   2. Look at the woman crossing the street: she's my French teacher!
   3. I've got an idea! Meet me in an hour in front of the school.
   4. My grandparents have got a house in Scotland.
2. **1.** Do you remember the name of the main actor in *Twilight*?
   2. I usually love Ø animals, but I hate the dog that my sister got for her birthday. He always barks at the people who are with her!
   3. I don't like Ø coffee, I prefer Ø tea.
   4. Ø English is a beautiful language.
3. Mot vertical : sportsmen ;
   singulier: sportsman
   (= un sportif).

					R	O	S	E	S	
				P	U	P	P	I	E	S
						B	O	Y	S	
			R	E	W	A	R	D	S	
				T	E	E	T	H		
					B	U	S	E	S	
							M	I	C	E
					F	E	E	T		
C	H	I	L	D	R	E	N			

4.

/s/	/iz/	/z/
cats, presents	pages, watches	girls, potatoes

Fiche 23 À ton tour !

1. 1. Did you have many problems there?
   2. Sorry, I'm busy. I don't have much time to talk to you.
   3. I'm lucky, there aren't many pupils in my class this year.
   4. She doesn't want to eat much (food). She doesn't feel very well.
2. 1. It was so cold that there were very few people in the street.
   2. There's too little chocolate left. We can't make cookies!
   3. She is very shy, she's got few friends.
   4. Few students study Korean at university.
   5. I'm sad to see he's making so little progress.
3. 1. You shouldn't drink so much coffee! Or you won't sleep tonight...
   2. There aren't many visitors today, we can stay in the park as long as we like.
   3. I'd like to make some brownies. I need some butter. Have you got any?
4. 1. My friends don't have any pets.
   2. There isn't any solution yet.
   3. I don't have any clue how to solve the problem.
   4. He didn't have any money at the time.

Fiche 24 À ton tour !

1. 1. Tony is on holiday with his family.
   2. Tony and his family are spending a few days in their house in Spain.
   3. We visited that museum with our class last year.
   4. Are you coming to the party with your sister ?
2. 1. a, d et e • 2. f et g • 3. b et c.
3. 1. Emily's bag is too heavy for her.
   2. James's (/iz/) computer is broken.
   3. My neighbours' house has been burgled.
   4. I can't find the children's ball.

Fiche 25 À ton tour !

1. 1. Her brother is older than her but he is as tall as her and he looks more childish.
   2. I think exercise 1 is more difficult than exercise 3 and it is less amusing!
   3. I am better at English than at Spanish, but I'm as good at Math as at Physics.
2. 1. New York is the largest and the most expensive city in the USA.
   2. The Lut desert in Iran is probably the hottest place on Earth.
   3. What is the easiest and the most comfortable way to travel between Paris and London?

3. Comparatifs : *bigger, happier, safer, nicer, better, farther, sadder.*

Superlatifs : *worst, furthest, tallest, slimmest, best, best.*

Superlatif caché : ugliest, superlatif de supériorité de l'adjectif ugly (*laid, moche*).

B	I	G	G	E	R	R	B	S
T	H	A	P	P	I	E	R	L
S	S	W	O	R	S	T	E	I
E	A	E	U	T	N	T	H	M
L	F	D	B	G	I	E	T	M
L	E	L	D	I	C	B	R	E
A	R	E	S	E	E	T	A	S
T	S	E	H	T	R	U	F	T

Fiche 26 Quiz express

1. Le pluriel des noms

1. two potatoes • **2.** two pencils • **3.** two phones • **4.** two women • **5.** two parties **6.** two brushes.

2. Les articles : *a, an, the* ou Ø

1. The teachers we have this year are quite nice.

2. His mother is an English teacher.

3. Ø French people aren't very good at languages.

4. The pupils in my class are very good at English.

3. Les quantifieurs

1. There were so many people at the concert that I couldn't see you.

2. Hurry up, please! I don't have much time!

3. There's too little time left! I can't finish tonight.

4. I'd like to make a few recommendations before I go.

5. Leave me alone! I don't need any help!

6. I'm sorry! There's no cake left.

4. La possession

1. Mr and Mrs Smith own this house: it's ~~his house~~ / their house / theirs.

2. I like Jane's jeans, but I don't like Tony's jeans: I prefer hers / ~~his jeans~~ / her jeans.

3. My sister's boyfriend looks like an actor. ~~His boyfriend~~ / Her boyfriend / he is so gorgeous!

5. Les comparatifs

Cars are faster than bikes.

Cars are more expensive than bikes.

Cars aren't as eco-friendly as bikes.

6. Les superlatifs

My father is older than my mother but he is more patient than her: he is the most patient person I know! My mother is very clever. I often tell her she's the most intelligent woman on earth! My older sister is the prettiest girl in the family. She is very nice, but not as nice as my brother Tim. Tim is the nicest boy and the best brother in the world! As for me, maybe I'm not the most wonderful daughter and sister you can dream of, but I know I'm lucky to have such a great family!

Fiche 27 À ton tour !

1. **1.** She's (is) swimming.
   2. He's (is) playing baseball.
   3. She's (is) dancing.
   4. He's (is) driving a/the bus.
2. **1.** People always drive on the left in England.
   2. Do you sometimes go to Britain?
   3. My brother doesn't often play tennis.
3. **1.** I don't think I can do it.
   2. Be quiet, please! My brother and sister are sleeping.
   3. Listen! She is playing the violin.
   4. I love this picture, all my family is smiling.
   5. He has football practice every Wednesday at 5 p.m.
   6. Gary doesn't like green beans very much.
   7. We are having vegetable soup for dinner tonight.

Fiche 28 À ton tour !

1. **1.** Last Saturday, Sebastian woke [verbe irrégulier] up at half past ten.
   2. After breakfast, he watched an episode of his favourite series on television.
   3. In the afternoon, he did [verbe irrégulier] his homework in his bedroom.
   4. At 4. pm, he met Alex on the tennis court. They played tennis for 2 hours.
2. **1.** I was hoping to get a new bike for my birthday, and I got one!
   2. I loved riding my bike when I was younger.
   3. At 10 a.m., he was riding his new bike.
   4. Look! He's riding his new bike! [le verbe est au présent en *be* + V-*ing* (*is riding*)]
3. **1.** Where did you go last summer?
   2. Was your sister working when you arrived?
   3. We didn't have time to do that yesterday. We'll do it tomorrow.
   4. Yesterday at 11p.m. ? They weren't doing anything! They were sleeping.
4. Last Sunday was my birthday and a beautiful day. So, we all decided to have lunch in the garden. But at the end of the meal, as my family and friends were

singing “Happy Birthday” and Mum was getting out of the kitchen with the beautiful cake she had made, there was a strong gust of wind and it suddenly started raining. The cake fell [verbe irrégulier] on the terrace floor and we all rushed inside the house! I was so disappointed!

Fiche 29 À ton tour !

1. 1. The plane has just landed.
   2. She has just missed the bus.
   3. The horse rider has just fallen from the/his horse.
   4. They've (have) just got married.
2. 1. My grandmother has lived in London all her life.
   2. My parents and I have been to Paris but we haven't visited the Eiffel Tower.
   3. Have you read J. K. Rowling's new book? • 4. What has she done again?
3. 1. for five hours.
   2. since he was born.
   3. since April 14th.
   4. for many years.
4. I've (already) played football but I've never played baseball. I've (already) painted. I've been to the USA. I've never eaten insects.
   [Bien sûr, ce ne sont que des exemples. Vérifie que tu as bien formé les participes passés et que tu as placé l'adverbe entre l'auxiliaire et le verbe.]

Fiche 30 À ton tour !

1. 1. Have you ever visited the Statue of Liberty? Yes, I visited it in August 2015.
   2. Have you ever driven a sports car? Yes, I drove one when I was in Le Mans last month.
   3. Have you ever played the guitar at a school concert? No, I've never played the guitar at a school concert.
2. 1. b : How long ago did you meet her?
   2. a : How long have you known her?
   3. e : I have never written a poem.
   4. d : Last night, I wrote a poem for you.
   5. f : We arrived here three years ago.
   6. c : We have lived here since 2012.
3. 1. My parents have been to a lot of countries but they have never been to New Zealand.
   2. My brother went to Iceland last year. He says it is the most beautiful place he has ever visited.
   3. This morning, I didn't hear my alarm clock! Of course, I missed my bus, and I arrived late at school.
   4. He has played the piano since he was 5 and he has always been very good at it.

Fiche 31 À ton tour !

1. **1.** passif • **2.** actif • **3.** actif • **4.** passif • **5.** actif.

2. **1.** This morning, Tony rode a/his bike [actif].
   2. When the rain started, Lana came home [actif].
   3. One hour ago, the burglar was arrested [passif].
   4. Yesterday Bobby was given a medal [passif].

3. **1.** Paper is made from wood.
   2. We are given a lot of homework (by our teachers).
   3. That won't be understood.
   4. *Hamlet* and *Romeo and Juliet* were written by Shakespeare.

Fiche 32 Quiz express

1. Présent simple ou présent en *be* + V-*ing* ?

1. I love going to the cinema.
2. Look at this picture! Everybody is smiling.
3. What are you doing now? • **4.** She isn't working today.
5. She doesn't usually work on Wednesdays.

2. Le prétérit simple

Il fallait rayer : **1.** he doesn't play • **2.** Do you go...? • **3.** they have been • **4.** Have you seen...?

3. Prétérit simple et prétérit *be* + V-*ing*?

1. He was running after the bus when I saw him.
2. They were sleeping when I left home this morning.
3. We last played tennis together two years ago.
4. I was making a cake when the bell rang.
5. When I arrived at the station, nobody was waiting for me.

4. Le *present perfect*

1. a • **2.** b • **3.** a.

5. *Present perfect* ou prétérit ?

1. I'm so happy I have finished my homework!
2. We have been in Paris since Monday but we haven't visited the Eiffel Tower yet.
3. They went to the Republic of Ireland in 2015 but they have never been to Northern Ireland.

6. Le passif

Slavery in America began when the first African slaves were brought to Virginia in 1619 and it was practiced almost everywhere in America in the 17th and 18th centuries. Slaves were owned by white masters and usually lived on farms or plantations under terrible conditions.

In the 19th century, a movement to abolish slavery grew in the North and divided the country. After the Civil War, millions of slaves were freed.

CORRIGÉS des quiz et des exercices

Fiche 33 À ton tour !

1. 1. My brother can't swim very well.
   2. I mustn't go out after 10. p.m.
   3. Can you help me ?
   4. They will have to stay there.
2. 1. I'm not able to speak Spanish.
   2. Am I allowed to open the window?
   3. It's forbidden to play ball in the classroom!
   4. They have to be on time.
3. 1. Yesterday, I had to go to the library to do some research on Charlotte Brontë.
   2. This morning, he wasn't able to log onto his computer.
   3. The headmaster said we were allowed to sit down.
   4. The policeman said we weren't allowed to park here.
   5. When I was young, I was able to run / I could run for two hours without stopping.

Fiche 34 À ton tour !

1. 1. capacité • 2. interdiction • 3. interdiction • 4. probabilité • 5. obligation • 6. capacité • 7. permission • 8. probabilité
2. You shouldn't sleep in class, you should listen to your teachers. You should go to bed early, you shouldn't play videogames late at night.
3. 1. She can paint extremely well. She's a real artist!
   2. It's very foggy tonight. You must drive carefully.
   3. We may get there on time, but I'm not sure.
   4. She might come with us, but we shouldn't count on her.
   5. Could you tell me the way to the cinema please?
4. 1. You can't / mustn't / ~~shouldn't~~ smoke here! It's forbidden. [interdiction]
   2. May / Could / ~~Must~~ I use your phone please? [demande de permission]
   3. You don't look very well. You must / ~~may~~ / should see a doctor. [ordre ou conseil]
   4. He ~~can't~~ / may / might be right but I don't know for sure. [probabilité]

Fiche 35 À ton tour !

1. 1. He's (is) going to leave.
   2. They're (are) going to cross the street.
   3. He's (is) going to fall.
   4. They're (are) going to play rugby.
2. 1. Are you going to go to London with us?
   2. What will you do tomorrow?
   3. My parents will not / won't come back tonight.
   4. I'm / am not going to stay here.

3. 1. If my parents agree, I'll go to Tom's party tonight.
2. Have you decided what you're going to do this summer?
3. I hope there will still be trees in 2500.

4. 1. My brother is going to get married this summer.
2. I'll (will) call you tomorrow morning.
3. If we go to London, we'll (will) visit Hyde Park.

Fiche 36 À ton tour !

1. 1. If my parents had more time, they'd (would) go on holiday.
2. If I met a star, I'd (would) take a picture.
3. If we were richer, we'd (would) give money to charities.
4. If Tony didn't have so much homework, he'd (would) go out with his friends.

2. 1. Mrs Reynold would like to go on holiday in the sun / to go to the beach.
2. She'd like Alex to go to the USA.
3. She'd like Chris to get married / to marry.
4. She'd like Celia to have a baby.

3. 1. c : If I were you, I wouldn't leave now.
2. d : You don't look very well, you should see a doctor.
3. a : Do you think you could help me for a few minutes?
4. b : I know you are hungry, would you like a sandwich?

4. 1. What could I do to help you?
2. You should go to the doctor's. You shouldn't wait.
3. I'd (would) be happy to see them.

Fiche 37 À ton tour !

1. 1. My parents don't let me Ø go to parties.
2. They told us to leave immediately!
3. My sister would like to study in the USA next year.
4. What do you expect me to do now?
5. She makes her children Ø walk the dog every day.

2. 1. The policeman wants the car / the driver to stop.
2. Ben's mother wants him to turn the music off/down.
3. The English teacher wants her students / pupils to speak English.
4. The children want the woman to give them sweets.

3. 1. b : She asked him to wait for her.
2. c : She can't bear waiting for him.
3. c : She left instead of waiting for him.
4. a : She always makes him wait for her.
5. b : She said she'd like him to wait for her.

4. 1. I don't like running (I don't like to run).
2. Stop talking! Work instead of chatting!
3. Travelling is always an interesting experience.

Fiche 38 Quiz express

1. Permission, obligation, interdiction

Il fallait rayer : **1.** b • **2.** a • **3.** c.

2. La probabilité

Il fallait entourer les phrases : 1, 2, 4.

3. *Be going to*

1. I • **2.** D [indice : he is carrying a suitcase] • **3.** D [jouer au ballon risque d'avoir pour conséquence de casser quelque chose] • **4.** I.

4. *Will* ou *be going to?*

1. I'm tired. I am going to go to bed.

2. Wait for me, I won't be long.

3. Look at that blue sky! It's going to be a beautiful day!

4. Luke will call you when he gets back from school.

5. Le conditionnel

1. d • **2.** c • **3.** b • **4.** e • **5.** a.

6. L'infinitif et le gérondif

1. Mum always makes me clear the table after dinner.

2. They never let us do what we want.

3. Parents want their children to work hard at school.

4. Please, stop complaining all the time!

5. Don't you think dancing is fun?

6. I need you to listen to me.

Fiche 39 À ton tour !

1. **1.** They weren't very shy at the time.

2. I haven't got a sister.

3. They aren't doing the washing-up.

4. She doesn't eat a lot of vegetables.

5. My grandparents didn't go to Mauritius last month.

2. **1.** b : Are you from Ireland? No, I'm not. I'm from Scotland.

2. a : Have you ever been to Scotland? Yes, I have. I went to Glasgow in 2014.

3. e : When did you visit Scotland? In 2014. I went to Edinburgh.

4. c : Where do you live? In Edinburgh, in Scotland.

5. d : When were you born? On June 30th 2006.

3. **1.** How old is your brother?

2. How many pupils are there in your class?

3. How long does it take to go to the shopping centre?

4. How tall is your father?

4. 1. "When do you go to the swimming pool?"

2. "Did you visit Buckingham Palace?"

Fiche 40 À ton tour !

1. 1. Is she ? • 2. Have you ? • 3. Can you ? • 4. Did you ?

2. 1. Tom is always very nice with her, isn't he?

2. Alex can play the guitar very well, can't he?

3. He hasn't played for long, has he?

4. The children should be more careful, shouldn't they?

5. Emma doesn't work on Wednesdays, does she?

3. 1. You're interested in languages, aren't you?

2. Your parents can't speak English, can they?

3. Your sister doesn't live with your family, does she?

4. She lives in the USA, doesn't she?

5. Your brother visited her last summer, didn't he?

4. 1. c : Have you got a few minutes to answer me? Yes, I have.

2. a : Are you a student here? Yes, I am.

3. b : Does your boyfriend go to the same school as you? No, he doesn't.

4. d : Do your friends often spend time with you? No, they don't.

5. f : Would the students here like to have more free time? Yes, they would.

Reste : e. La question commence par *Did* + sujet à la 3e pers. du pl. : Did they have a good time at school today? Did your friends go to the cinema last weekend?...

Fiche 41 À ton tour !

1. 1. The history courses I take are so interesting! My history teacher is such a fascinating man!

2. I've had such a good time in London! I've never had such fun! I'm so happy!

3. My neighbours are such strange people! I feel so uncomfortable when I meet them!

2. What a complicated story! What an enormous cake you've made! What eccentric clothes she's wearing today! • How pretty she is! How quickly you did your homework!

3. 1. How awesome (this is)! / This is so awesome!

2. What a nice view (we have from here)! / We're having such a nice view!

3. What a beautiful city! / London is such a beautiful city!

4. How high we are! /We are so high!

5. What impressive buildings (we can see from here)! / The Houses of parliament are / We can see such impressive buildings!

4. 1. How tall your father is!

2. How tall are you?

3. What present will you bring her for her birthday?

4. What nice presents she got for her birthday!

5. How expensive these jeans are!

Fiche 42 À ton tour !

1. 1. who • 2. which • 3. which • 4. who.

2. Sont à rayer : 1. which • 2. who • 3. Ø • 4. Aucun relatif n'est à rayer • 5. who • 6. Ø.

3. 1. The children I looked after last weekend are very polite.

2. The exam we're talking about is really difficult.

3. The school my grandmother studied in is a very old building.

4. 1. Ray whose car is parked in front of the school has come to drive us back home.

2. I have never met the man whose wife is a famous actress.

3. Cathy whose family I don't know yet lives just next door.

Fiche 43 Quiz express

1. Les phrases interrogatives

1. Where • 2. How many • 3. Whose • 4. How often.

2. Les phrases négatives

1. b • 2. c • 3. a • 4. e.

3. Les *question tags*

1. You don't really like French, do you?

2. Tom goes to school at 8 a.m, doesn't he?

3. His parents lived abroad for two years, didn't they?

4. Olivia will come with us, won't she?

5. They haven't seen her for weeks, have they?

4. Les réponses brèves

Les réponses brèves qui ne conviennent pas sont : 1. c • 2. a • 3. b • 4. a.

5. Les subordonnées relatives

1. Do you know the boy who takes the bus with us every Monday?

2. Do you know the man whose wife is a Scottish writer?

3. The book Ø I have just read is fantastic!

4. The phone which has been left on the desk is probably the teacher's.

5. He's the guy Ø she fell in love with.

6. All that glitters is not gold.

MÉMO grammatical

Les pronoms personnels

		sujets	compléments	réfléchis
singulier	1re pers.	I	me	myself
	2e pers.	you	you	yourself
	3e pers. masculin féminin neutre	he she it	him her it	himself herself itself
pluriel	1re pers.	we	us	ourselves
	2e pers.	you	you	yourselves
	3e pers.	they	them	themselves

Les possessifs

▶ Parmi les possessifs, on distingue les adjectifs, qui sont suivis d'un nom (*it's* ***my*** *bag*) et les pronoms, qui remplacent le nom (*this bag is* ***mine***).

		adjectifs	pronoms
singulier	1re pers.	my	mine
	2e pers.	your	yours
	3e pers. masculin féminin neutre	his her its	his hers its
pluriel	1re pers.	our	ours
	2e pers.	your	yours
	3e pers.	their	theirs

Les mots interrogatifs

▶ Les principaux mots interrogatifs

what	*que ? quoi ? ...*	What are you doing?
which	*quel (quelle...) ?* *lequel (laquelle...) ?*	Which book do you prefer?
who	*qui ?*	Who is your best friend?
whose	*à qui ?*	Whose bag is it?
when	*quand ?*	When are the next holidays?
where	*où ?*	Where do you live?
why	*pourquoi ?*	Why are you laughing?
how	*comment ?*	How do you say that in English?

▶ Les mots interrogatifs avec *how*

how much (seul)	*combien ?* [prix]	How much are these shoes?
how much (+ sg.) how many (+ pl.)	*combien ?* [quantité]	How much time do you need? How many people did you meet?
how often	*à quelle fréquence ?*	How often do you go to the gym?
how long	*combien de temps ?*	How long did he stay there?
how old	*quel âge ?*	How old is your sister?
how far	*à quelle distance?*	How far is the city centre?

Les nombres

Cardinaux	
1	one
2	two
3	three
4	four
5	five
6	six
7	seven
8	eight
9	nine
10	ten
11	eleven
12	twelve
13	thirteen
14	fourteen
15	fifteen
16	sixteen
17	seventeen
18	eighteen
19	nineteen
20	twenty
21	twenty-one
22	twenty-two
30	thirty
40	forty
50	fifty
60	sixty
70	seventy
80	eighty
90	ninety
100	a/one hundred
1000	a/one thousand

Ordinaux	
1st	first
2nd	second
3rd	third
4th	fourth
5th	fifth
6th	sixth
7th	seventh
8th	eighth
9th	nineth
10th	tenth
11th	eleventh
12th	twelfth
13th	thirteenth
14th	fourteenth
15th	fifteenth
16th	sixteenth
17th	seventeenth
18th	eighteenth
19th	nineteenth
20th	twentieth
21st	twenty-first
22nd	twenty-second
30th	thirtieth
40th	fortieth
50th	fiftieth
60th	sixtieth
70th	seventieth
80th	eightieth
90th	ninetieth
100th	hundredth
1000th	thousandth

Les quantifieurs

▶ Une certaine quantité

quantité positive	some	There are some books on your desk. [on ne sait pas combien, mais on sait qu'il y en a]
quantité inconnue	any	Are there any books on your desk? [on ne sait pas s'il y en a]
quantité nulle	not... any no	There aren't any books on your desk. There are no books on your desk.

▶ Une grande ou une petite quantité

grande quantité	much (+ sg.) many (+ pl.) a lot of, lots of	There isn't much time left. There are many books on your desk. I don't have a lot of time / a lot of books.
quantité excessive	too much (+sg.) too many (+ pl.)	You gave me too much money! There are too many books on your desk.
petite quantité	a little (+ sg.) a few (+ pl.)	There is a little time left, no need to hurry. There are a few books on your desk.
quantité insuffisante	little (+ sg.) few (+ pl.)	There is little time left, hurry up! Good job, there are very few mistakes!

▶ La plupart, la totalité

tout(e), tou(te)s	all	All the books are on your desk. Stop complaining all the time!
chaque, chacun(e)	every ou each	I go to school every day [chaque jour = tous les jours] but each day is different [chaque jour = chacun de ces jours].
la plupart	most (+ N) most of (+ déterm. ou pronom)	Most students / Most of the students passed the test.

MÉMO grammatical

Conjuguer *be* au présent et au prétérit

▶ Forme affirmative : **sujet + *be* conjugué**

	présent	prétérit
I	am ('m)	was
we, you, they	are ('re)	were
he/she/it	is ('s)	was

▶ Forme interrogative : ***be* conjugué + sujet** (*Am I? Was I?*)

▶ Forme négative : **sujet + *be* conjugué + *not*** (*I am not, I was not*)
À l'oral, on utilise souvent une forme contractée :

	présent	prétérit
I	am not ('m not)	wasn't
we, you, they	are not ('re / aren't)	weren't
he/she/it	is not ('s not / isn't)	wasn't

Conjuguer *have* et *have got*

▶ *Have* (présent) :

Forme affirmative	Forme négative	Forme interrogative
I, we, you, they have	I, we, you, they don't have	Do I have... ?
he/she/it has	he/she/it doesn't have	Does he have... ?

▶ *Have got (present perfect)* :

Forme affirmative	Forme négative	Forme interrogative
I, we, you, they have got	I, we, you, they haven't got	Have I got... ?
he/she/it has got	he/she/it hasn't got	Has he got... ?

Les modaux : *can, could, may, must…*

▶ Caractéristiques :

- identiques à toutes les personnes ;
- toujours suivis d'une base verbale, jamais d'un autre modal ;
- se conjuguent sans *do* aux formes interrogative et négative.

▶ Construction :

- forme affirmative : **sujet + modal** + BV
- forme négative : **sujet + modal + *not*** + BV
- forme interrogative : **modal + sujet** + BV

→ I can do what I want.
→ I can't do what I want.
→ Can I do what I want?

▶ Valeur des modaux et formes verbales équivalentes

	présent	passé	futur
capacité	can	could	will be able to
incapacité	can't	couldn't	won't be able to
permission	can may	could was/were allowed to	will be allowed to
obligation	must	had to	will have to
interdiction	can't mustn't	couldn't was/were not allowed to	won't be allowed to

Conjuguer un verbe régulier : *play*

▶ Forme affirmative :

	sujet	auxiliaire	verbe
présent simple	I, we, you, they		play
	he/she/it		plays
présent en *be* + *V-ing*	I	am	playing
	he/she/it	is	
	we, you, they	are	
prétérit	I, he/she/it, we, you, they		played
present perfect	I, we, you, they	have	played
	he/she/it	has	

▶ Forme interrogative :

	auxiliaire	sujet	verbe
présent simple	do	I, we, you, they	play?
	does	he/she/it	
présent en *be* + *V-ing*	am	I	playing?
	is	he/she/it	
	are	we, you, they	
prétérit	did	I, he/she/it, we, you, they	play?
present perfect	have	I, we, you, they	played?
	has	he/she/it	

▶ Forme négative :

	sujet	auxiliaire + *not*	verbe
présent simple	I, we, you, they	do not (don't)	play
	he/she/it	does not (doesn't)	
présent en *be* + *V-ing*	I	am not ('m not)	playing
	he/she/it	is not (isn't)	
	we, you, they	are not (aren't)	
prétérit	I, he/she/it, we, you, they	did not (didn't)	play
present perfect	I, we, you, they	have not (haven't)	played
	he/she/it	has not (hasn't)	

Conjuguer un verbe irrégulier : *eat*

▶ Forme affirmative :

	sujet	auxiliaire	verbe
présent simple	I, we, you, they		eat
	he/she/it		eats
présent en *be* + *V-ing*	I	am	eating
	he/she/it	is	
	we, you, they	are	
prétérit	I, he/she/it, we, you, they		ate
present perfect	I, we, you, they	have	eaten
	he/she/it	has	

▶ Forme interrogative :

	auxiliaire	sujet	verbe
présent simple	do	I, we, you, they	eat?
	does	he/she/it	
présent en *be* + *V-ing*	am	I	eating?
	is	he/she/it	
	are	we, you, they	
prétérit	did	I, he/she/it, we, you, they	eat?
present perfect	have	I, we, you, they	eaten?
	has	he/she/it	

▶ Forme négative :

	sujet	auxiliaire + *not*	verbe
présent simple	I, we, you, they	do not (don't)	eat
	he/she/it	does not (doesn't)	
présent en *be* + *V-ing*	I	am not ('m not)	eating
	he/she/it	is not (isn't)	
	we, you, they	are not (aren't)	
prétérit	I, he/she/it, we, you, they	did not (didn't)	eat
present perfect	I, we, you, they	have not (haven't)	eaten
	he/she/it	has not (hasn't)	

INDEX des podcats

Compréhension orale

Expression orale

Focus

INDEX des thèmes de vocabulaire

Crédits iconographiques

8	ph © Michael Reaves / Getty-Images / AFP
10	ph © Yale Center for British Art, Paul Mellon Collection, USA / Bridgeman Images
12	ph © Image Source / Getty-Images
14	Coll. Christophel © R.P. Productions / Runteam Ltd
30	© D.R.
32	ph © Granger Coll NY / Aurimages
34	ph © Gregg Vignal / Alamy Stock Photo
38 h	ph © The National Archives / SSPL / Getty-Images
38 b	ph © Bear66 / Dreamstime.com
92	© creativecommons.org
93	ph © jorisvo/Shutterstock
95	ph © ChameleonsEye/Shutterstock
96	ph © Photo12/Alamy
99	ph © bhofack2 / iStock
100	ph ©Brandon Bourdages / Shutterstock

N° imprimeur : 2017051203
Dépôt légal n° 03214-9/01 - Juin 2017
Achevé d'imprimer en France par LOIRE OFFSET TITOULET